The Works of John Sheffield

by John Sheffield Buckingham (Duke Of)

Address:
HardPress
8345 NW 66TH ST #2561
MIAMI FL 33166-2626
USA
Email: info@hardpress.net

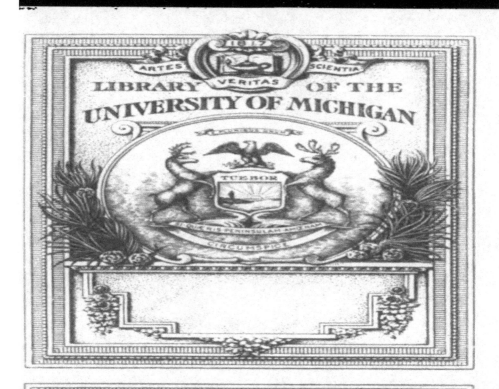
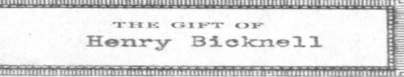

Henry Bicknell.

THE
WORKS

OF

JOHN SHEFFIELD,

EARL of MULGRAVE,

MARQUIS of NORMANBY,

AND

Duke of *BUCKINGHAM.*

VOL. II.

𝕿𝕳𝖊 𝕾𝖊𝖈𝖔𝖓𝖉 𝕰𝖉𝖎𝖙𝖎𝖔𝖓 𝕮𝖔𝖗𝖗𝖊𝖈𝖙𝖊𝖉.

LONDON,

Printed for **J. B.** and fold by **AARON WARD**, at the *King's Arms,* in *Little-Britain*; **T. WOTTON**, at the *Three Daggers and Queen's-head,* againft *St. Dunftan's* Church, *Fleet-ftreet*; **D. BROWNE**, at the *Black Swan,* without *Temple-Bar*; **R. WILLIAMSON**, at *Grey's-Inn Gate, Holborn*; **T. ASTLEY**, at the *Rofe,* in *St. Paul's Church-yard*; and **J. STAGE** in *Weftminfter-Hall.*

M.DCC.XXIX.

(iii)

The TABLE.

VOL. II.

(iv)

MEMOIRS

OF

HIS GRACE

JOHN

Duke of *Buckingham*.

Written by Himfelf.

VOL. II.   B

MEMOIRS.

 AVING obſerved that Memoirs and Accounts of perſons tho' not very conſiderable, when written by themſelves, have been greedily read, and often found uſeful; not only for the knowledge of things paſt, but as cautions for the fu-

ture;

ture : I have chofen to imploy fome part of that leifure (which I have had by intervals, and which by reafon of decaying health and vigour I know not how to fpend better) in fetting down exactly and impartially all I could remember of my felf, fit to be made publick ; a kind of picture left behind me to my friends and family, very like, tho' neither well painted, nor handfome.

I fhall begin it at the age of feventeen ; when hearing every where the Earl of Ossory commended, for being a Voluntier that fummer in a hot engagement at fea ; I went thither directly, on board that fhip, in which Prince RUPERT and the Duke of ALBEMARLE jointly commanded the Fleet againft the *Dutch*.

THEIR ufage of me was fo civil, and the company on board them fo good : that (tho' by a fudden ftorm that parted the two Fleets juft ready to engage, I loft fix weeks time there, at an age when it may be a great deal more pleafantly fpent) yet I ftay'd 'till the Fleet was laid up, not only without impatience, but any fort of uneafinefs.

YET 'tis obfervable, that the firft night we came to *London*, the Lord BLANY, Sir THOMAS CLIFFORD afterwards Lord Treafurer,

Mr.

Mr. HENRY SAVILL, and my felf (tho' fuch
familiar friends, as to be very often together
for many years after) were then fo fatiated and
cloy'd with each other by our being fhut up
together fo long in one fhip, that I remember
we avoided one another's company at leaft for
a whole month after; tho' except my felf,
there could hardly be any more pleafant.

WHILE I was in that fhip with Prince
RUPERT and the Duke of ALBEMARLE, I
obferved the latter to leave all things to the
conduct and skill of the other; declaring
modeftly upon all occafions himfelf to be
no Seaman. And yet there happened once
a hot difpute between them, which will
fhew fome part of that Duke's character.
When we firft efpied the *Dutch* fleet failing
towards us, our whole blue fquadron was
aftern much farther from us; fo that Prince
RUPERT thought it abfolutely neceffary to
flacken fail, that they might have time to
join us. But the Duke of ALBEMARLE oppofed it eagerly; undertaking that the fhip
in which they were, with about twenty
fhips more, would prove fufficient to beat
all the enemies fleet; at leaft, hold them in
play 'till the reft of ours came up. The Prince,
aftonifhed at fuch an unaccountable intrepi-

dity, made us smile to see him take on himself the timorous, cautious, and prudential
part, which did not use to be his custom;
he declared he would never consent to such
a rashness as might very probably cost us the
loss of our Admiral's ship, and consequently
of our whole fleet afterwards; which obliged the good old man to yield at last, but
with a great deal of reluctance.

As soon as the bloody flag was set up,
before the storm arose which parted us,
Mr. SAVILL and my self being on the quarter-
deck, 'spied him charging a very little pis-
tol, and putting it in his pocket : which was
so odd a sort of a weapon on such an occasion, that we two could imagine no reason for it, except his having taken a resolution of going down into the powder-room
to blow up the ship, in case at any time it
should be in danger of being taken : For
he had often said he would answer for nothing, but that we should never be carried
into *Holland :* and therefore Mr. SAVILL
and I, in a laughing way, most mutinously
resolved to throw him overboard, in case
we should ever catch him going down to
the powder-room.

Our fleet happening afterwards to go
near the shore to take in fresh water, Prince
RU-

RUPERT dined with a gentleman who lived thereabouts ; and returning on board in a little boat with only the Lord BLANY and my felf, there happened fo fudden and violent a ftorm, that we did not like it ; and Prince RUPERT began to talk of Prince MAURICE's being caft away by a like accident ; upon which, I could not but reflect on my family alfo, fince my grandfather and three of his brothers had been drowned. The Lord BLANY hearing all this, made us fmile in the midft of our danger, by fwearing, that tho' he liked our company, he wifh'd himfelf out of it, and in any other boat whatfoever ; fince he feared the ill fortune of our two families wou'd fink him.

THIS was the laft year of the firft *Dutch* War ; yet before it ended, they burnt fome of our beft fhips at *Chatham*, and defign'd to make a defcent upon our coafts ; which occafion'd the raifing of feveral independent troops of horfe ; of which I had one given me, and was fo foolifhly fond of it, (being my firft military command) that I indured my quarters at *Dover* as contentedly, and was as forry for being disbanded upon the Peace, as if I had been a meer foldier of fortune.

AT

AT the next meeting of Parliament, I receiv'd a writ to fit there ; and being known by every body to be younger by three years than the prefixed age for the voting in the *House of Peers*, it was oppofed by ALGERNOON Earl of NORTHUMBERLAND, who very gravely moved, that they would rather exclude Lords till fome years above the age of one and twenty, inftead of admitting one fo much younger. In this he certainly was in the right ; and I acquiefced in it the more willingly, becaufe that heat of youth (which was his objection) made me a great deal more inclined to fomething elfe, than to fitting there. Accordingly I followed it with too much eagernefs, and without interruption, 'till the fecond *Dutch* war : During this time, and heat of temper, I had the good fortune not to be ingaged in more than one quarrel ; but that had fomewhat in it fingular enough to be related. I was informed that the Earl of ROCHESTER had faid fomething of me, which, according to his cuftom, was very malicious ; I therefore fent Colonel ASTON, a very mettled friend of mine, to call him to account for it. He denied the words, and indeed I was foon convinced he had never faid them ; but the

meer

meer report, tho' I found it to be falfe, obliged me (as I then foolifhly thought) to go
on with the quarrel; and the next day was
appointed for us to fight on horfeback, a
way in *England* a little unufual, but it was
his part to chufe. Accordingly I and my
Second lay the night before at *Knightsbridge*
privately, to avoid the being fecured at *London* upon any fufpicion; which yet we found
our felves more in danger of there, becaufe
we had all the appearance of Highway-men
that had a mind to lie skulking in an odd
Inn, for one night; but this I fuppofe the
people of that houfe were ufed to, and fo
took no notice of us, but liked us the better. In the morning we met the Lord Ro-
CHESTER at the place appointed, who, inftead of JAMES PORTER whom he affured
ASTON he would make his Second, brought
an errant Life-guard-man whom no body
knew. To this Mr. ASTON took exception,
upon the account of his being no fuitable
adverfary; efpecially confidering how extreamly well he was mounted, whereas we
had only a couple of pads: Upon which,
we all agreed to fight on foot. But, as my
Lord ROCHESTER and I were riding into the
next field in order to it, he told me, that he
had

had at firſt choſen to fight on horſeback, becauſe he was ſo weak with a certain diſtem-
per, that he found himſelf unfit to fight at
all any way, much leſs a-foot. I was extreamly ſurpriz'd, becauſe at that time no
man had a better reputation for courage; and
(my anger againſt him being quite over, becauſe I was ſatisfied that he never ſpoke thoſe
words I reſented) I took the liberty of re-
preſenting what a ridiculous ſtory it would
make, if we returned without fighting; and
therefore adviſed him for both our ſakes,
eſpecially for his own, to conſider better of
it; ſince I muſt be obliged in my own defence to lay the fault on him by telling the
truth of the matter. His anſwer was, that
he ſubmitted to it; and hoped that I would
not deſire the advantage of having to do
with any man in ſo weak a condition. I
replied, that by ſuch an argument he had
ſufficiently tied my hands, upon condition I
might call our Seconds to be witneſſes of
the whole buſineſs; which he conſented to,
and ſo we parted. When we returned to
London, we found it full of this quarrel,
upon our being abſent ſo long; and therefore Mr. AſTON thought himſelf obliged to
write down every word and circumſtance of
this

this whole matter, in order to spread every where the true reason of our returning without having fought; which being never in the least either contradicted or resented by the Lord ROCHESTER, intirely ruined his reputation as to Courage, (of which I was really sorry to be the occasion) tho' no body had still a greater as to Wit; which supported him pretty well in the world, notwithstanding some more accidents of the same kind, that never fail to succeed one another when once people know a man's weakness.

WITHIN a few years after, a war against the *Dutch* was again declared, tho' not 'till a squadron of our ships had endeavoured to intercept and surprise their *Smyrna* fleet a little unfairly: of which design we failed very oddly, and by a fault that had certainly been punished under a wise administration. Sir EDWARD SPRAGG, who heard nothing of the war, returned home in company with those very *Smyrna* merchants: and with his whole squadron sailing faster than they, passed by ours that lay in wait for them; and yet Sir ROBERT HOLMES, our commander, and alone trusted with the secret, would not so much as communicate it to Sir EDWARD

SPRAGG,

SPRAGG, becauſe he muſt have commanded both ſquadrons (as being the ſuperiour officer) and conſequently deprive him of a prize, which, inſtead of that, proved an errant Tartar: For the *Smyrna* merchants, together with their *Dutch* convoy, made their part good againſt Sir ROBERT HOLMES's ſquadron; and ſo got ſafe home, meerly for want of Sir EDWARD SPRAGG's being called to his aſſiſtance.

THE Duke of YORK, always eager after a military fame, and Admiral of *England,* commanded the fleet in perſon that ſummer: which made me go a Voluntier once more, tho' I confeſs not with half ſo good a will as before; my heart being ingaged violently at that time, and I can never forget the tenderneſs of our parting.

I waited on the Duke in his own ſhip, where I intended to ſtay; but meeting the Earl of OSSORY there, who was both my kinſman and friend, and commanded the *Victory,* a Second-rate ſhip; he invited me ſo earneſtly to be with him, that I accepted his kindneſs; and afterwards found I could not have been any where elſe ſo well, on ſeveral accounts; ſince no man

ever

ever did more bravely than he, on all occasions.

SOON after, I had some experience of
the Duke's firmness in any resolution he had
once taken; for tho' he grew so very kind
to me, as to favour me in much greater
matters, yet I could never prevail on him
to grant me one request, which at that time
I thought it a little hard to be denied. My
request was, that if in the next ingagement
he perceived any ship to fail of doing its
duty, by reason of her Captain's being killed
(which was but too usual) he would then
send me an order to go on board and command her immediately; whereby, instead of
being an insignificant Voluntier, I might have
an opportunity of doing the fleet some service, and of gaining some honour. But
tho' he knew it well, and allowed the reason of the thing, as being the only way of
making the Voluntiers useful; yet he counted it too great an alteration of the settled
orders, which gave the Lieutenant in such
a case the same power which his Captain before had, tho' seldom found to make good
use of it.

OUR

OUR scouts having been negligent, DE RUITER with his whole fleet surprized ours at *South-wold Bay*; so that weighing anchor in great haste, we had much ado to defend our selves from their Fire-ships: DE RUITER himself was seen nobly to go in a boat from ship to ship, to direct and animate his men, ordering all his ships to attack only our great ones; which, not being much above twenty, were hard put to it by so great a number of theirs. Yet the enemy had no success to boast of, except the burning our *Royal James*; which, having on board her, not only a thousand of our best men, but the Earl of SANDWYCH himself Vice-Admiral of *England*, was enough almost to stile it a victory on their side, since his merit as to sea-affairs was most extraordinary in all kinds. He dined in Mr. DIGBY's ship the day before the battle, when no body dreamt of fighting, and shewed a gloomy discontent so contrary to his usual chearful humour, that we even then all took notice of it; but much more, afterwards.

THE enemy also was once master of the *Royal Katherine*, and had sent away her Captain Sir JOHN CHICHELY with most of

her

her men, to be kept prisoners in other ships; a few only remaining there, whom they stowed under hatches, with a guard over them. But the boatswain being among them, with his whistle encouraged the rest to knock down all the sentinels first, and then to fall on the *Dutch* above deck; by which brisk action they redeemed that considerable ship. The boatswain's name was SMALL, whom I had opportunity of knowing well afterwards when I had the command of that ship. He was a *Nonconformist*, always sober, meek, and quiet, (even too mild for that bustling sort of employment) and very often gave me an image of those enthusiastick people who did such brave things in our late *Civil War*: for he seemed rather a Shepherd than a Soldier; and was a kind of heroe in the shape of a saint.

BUT the Duke of YORK himself had the noblest share in this day's action; for, when his ship was so maim'd as to be made incapable of service, he made her lie by, to refit, and went on board another that was hotly engaged, where he kept up his standard 'till she was disabled also; and then left her for a third, in order to renew the fight, which

which lasted from break of day till sun-set. About which time, the whole *French* squadron happen'd to sail close by the Lord OSSORY's ship ; and I well remember there did not appear so many shot in them all, as in his Lordship's single ship ; whose condition therefore was judged too bad to keep the sea any longer.   I then found by experience in this engagement, how much there is of custom in the matter of courage, which makes old troops so formidable : for in the morning when the enemy's great shot came on both sides of us, I thought it impossible to 'scape without losing a limb at least, and was accordingly pretty uneasy ; but, about the afternoon, when the broad-sides came only one way, though without interruption, I began to grow a little less sensible of the danger, which yet I was very glad to see ended at night.   By that time I was very sufficiently tired ; but yet had much ado to sleep, by reason of the noise still sounding in my ears ; which remained so for some hours, just as if the shooting had still continued.   I observed also two things, which I dare affirm, tho' not generally believ'd. One was, that the wind of a cannon-bullet,

tho'

tho' flying never fo near, is incapable of doing the leaft harm; and indeed, were it otherwife, no man above deck would e- fcape. The other was, that a great fhot may be fometimes avoided even as it flies, by changing one's ground a little; for, when the wind fometimes blew away the fmoak, it was fo clear a fun-fhiny day, that we could eafily perceive the bullets (that were half fpent) fall in the water, and from thence bound up again among us; which gives fuffi- cient time for making a ftep or two on any fide; tho' in fo fwift a motion, 'tis hard to judge well in what line the bullet comes; which, if miftaken, may by removing coft a man his life, inftead of faving it.

As foon as I came to *London,* (whi- ther I made all the hafte imaginable for reafons not hard to guefs) I found by my reception every where, that my Lord OSSORY's kind and partial Letters had ar- rived there before me; for the King made me fome particular complements, and offer- ed me the choice of commanding the *Henry* or the *Royal Katherine;* the Cap- tain of the firft having been killed, and the other taken prifoner. I chofe the *Katherine;* and, fince I had been fo fond of a troop of

horfe,

horfe, 'tis no wonder I was now extreamly
pleafed with the command of a royal fhip,
better in all refpects than my Lord OSSORY'S,
and of a rate above what I could have pretended to; for even he, who was fo much
more confiderable on all accounts, had only
a third rate fhip granted him at firft, whereas the *Katherine* was then the beft of all
the fecond rates.

M E.

MEMOIRS

In the R E I G N of

CHARLES II.

G 2

CAROLUS · II · D · G · ANGL · SCOT · FRAN · ET · HIB · REX ·

MEMOIRS

In the REIGN of

CHARLES II.

HAVE found much more satisfaction, and, I may say, instruction too, from those small pieces of history called *Memoirs*, than in reading all the *Greek* and *Roman* historians : the reason of which would

require a digreffion too long for this place.
But my own experience of this, is fufficient
to make me do as I would be done by, in
a matter fo eafy for me; and to give as
particular an account of fome few things I
know, as I fhould be glad to have from
others, about thofe many confiderable affairs of which I am ignorant.

THAT which confirms me in the opinion,
that even this flight account will be in fome
meafure ufeful, is the exact impartiality I
am refolved to obferve in it. Tho', i confefs, it remained a difficulty with me, a good
while, how to lay afide intirely, not only
my inclinations, but my obligations alfo ;
which latter, methought, it was a kind of
ingratitude to fufpend the thoughts of, tho'
but for a moment : Yet, without doing this,
I thought it would be as ridiculous to write
(tho' like moft other authors) as to publifh
my dreams, or expofe all the follies of my
own paffions.

NOTWITHSTANDING this, I would
not have all I fay, taken for infallible, except only the matters of fact. For, as to the
defigns of men, and the true reafons of their
acting, affairs of this world are like a dye,
with many fides on it, and one gamefter
                                        can

can only fee thofe which are turn'd towards him. But then, if others would difcover as much, we might hope the true *Memoirs,* would make a little amends for the frequent *perjuries,* of our times; and in thofe at leaft we might find the truth, the whole truth, and nothing but the truth.

IN the year 1672, Monfieur DE SCHOM_ BERG was invited into *England,* to command the new-raifed army incamped on *Black-heath,* which at firft was under the * Duke of BUCKINGHAM only, who had a com-miffion of Lieutenant-General. But he be-ing no great foldier, and on ill terms with the Duke of YORK, who influenced all our military affairs at that time, it was thought convenient to join with him a perfon of fuch reputation as SCHOMBERG. And he was chofen the rather, becaufe his advancement in *France,* next to his own good conduct, was owing chiefly to the Duke of YORK, when in that fervice: For by the ancient treaties between *France* and *Scotland,* the Duke of ALBANY having always the difpofal of their *Scotch* Guards; the *French* King made him the complement of leaving the commander of them to his choice, which he fixed on Monfieur DE SCHOMBERG.

* GEORGE VILLERS Duke of *Buckingham.*

C 4

As

As foon as he arrived, partly on account of his great reputation and fuccefs in *Portugal*, and partly incouraged to it by his friends, or rather the Duke of BUCKINGHAM's enemies, he refufed to ferve equally with him, and fo obtained a commiffion to be General; upon which, as was expected, the other quitted the fervice immediately.

JUST at this time the Duke of MONMOUTH was fetting up in *France* to be a foldier; and being fo favoured at *Maeftrich* by the *French* King, as to have a fure and eafy attacque kept back on purpofe 'till his day came of commanding; the credit here of that action, (tho' only a noble fort of prefent from that Prince's generofity and friendfhip for his Father) fufficed to give him a reputation ever after. Our fleet was now ready to fail, together with the new-raifed army, to make a defcent in *Holland*; the whole commanded in chief by Prince RUPERT, with the title of Generaliffimo.

I am apt to believe there never was feen before fo great a fleet, as this of ours when the *French* fquadron join'd with it; convoying 8000 Land-foldiers all fhipp'd in fmall veffels, which was fome addition to

the

the magnificence of so terrible, and yet so goodly a spectacle.

THE reason why the Duke of YORK, whose heart was set on such things, did not shine as the year before, at the head of all these troops, was his refusing the Test passed in Parliament the last winter on purpose to exclude him; so that, as soon as ever his enemies had set the snare, he fell into it.

THE *Greyhound*, being the best of those small vessels which accompanied the fleet, was chosen by Monsieur DE SCHOMBERG for himself and me, who happened to serve in that expedition under him, and with whom I had the good fortune to live in some familiarity and friendship.

THERE being often occasion of our speaking with other officers, who, in hazy-weather especially, were at a loss sometimes how to find out the *Greyhound* in the midst of such a multitude of other ships; Monsieur DE SCHOMBERG inquired of me one day, if it might not be proper to hang up something for a signal, by which all the Land-officers might know whither to repair, either to give account of their condition, or to receive his orders. I presently answered, that, tho'

last

laft fummer I had the honour of commanding a great fhip, yet I was but a young Seaman; and therefore only advifed him to
confult with CLEMENT the captain of the
Greyhound, who by right alfo was to be
principally regarded in his own fhip.   Captain CLEMENT was fent for, and prefently
confented to a thing which he thought not
only reafonable but neceffary to prevent delays or miftakes: which made the General,
according to his accuftomed civility, ask my
confent to hang up in the fhrouds one of
the colours of my own regiment that happened to lie then on the deck; faying
that he chofe fuch a fort of fignal, as more
proper for him to make ufe of, than any of
thofe which belonged to the Sea.   But it
had not been fet up half an hour, when
both of us fitting together on the quarter-
deck, heard a bullet whizzing over our heads,
and another in the fame manner prefently
after; at which we began to think cannon
bullets that came fo near a little worth the
minding; but were extremely furprized to
perceive they came from the Admiral.

By this time Captain CLEMENT was a-
larmed alfo; and he confirming the General's apprehenfion of Prince RUPERT's difli-
king

king his fignal, was fent immediately to explain the occafion of its being fet up, and to receive the Prince's orders either in that or any thing elfe, which fhould inftantly be obeyed.

But the Prince in the mean time fent Lieutenant WHITLY with his pofitive command to pull down the flag; who arriving on board the *Greyhound* juft after Captain CLEMENT had been fent away, it was thought fo impoffible for the Prince to remain unfatisfied after he fhould hear CLEMENT about it, that WHITLY was defired to return with this refpectful anfwer, That if his Highnefs continued in the fame mind after hearing the occafion from Captain CLEMENT, the flag fhould be taken down immediately. But the Prince, feeing WHITLY's boat come from the *Greyhound* without the flag's being taken down, and Captain CLEMENT juft arrived on board him, in great anger orders him to be clapp'd into the bilboes, without fo much as hearing either him, or his meffage: and commanded his Gunner to fink the *Greyhound* immediately if the flag was not taken down.

In fuch a cafe of extremity, the Voluntiers of quality on board the Prince took
the

the liberty of interpoſing a little, and con-
jured him to have only the patience of letting ſome of them go preſently to the *Grey-*
hound, in order to prevent any miſunder-
ſtanding; conſidering that ſome allowance
might be made for a miſtake in a land-officer
and a ſtranger.   It was not hard for perſons
of that rank (among whom was the Earl of
CARLISLE, a Privy Counſellor, and what
was more, a great friend of the Prince's) to
be connived at in going immediately on
board the *Greyhound;* and it was as eaſy
for them to perſuade us all immediately to
pull down our flag rather than be ſunk.   But
neither they, nor I, who was a little concerned with him in the ill uſage, were able
to pacify the General; who interpreted all
this harſh way of proceeding, as coming
from an old pique in Prince RUPERT, who
was too well-bred otherwiſe to uſe an old
acquaintance and a foreigner in ſuch a bru-
tal manner, as he called it.

THE Court was inclined before, not to
be over-partial to Prince RUPERT, who
ſeem'd as jealous as any body of its grow-
ing arbitrary by any great ſucceſs over *Hol-*
land, though himſelf was Generaliſſimo a-
gainſt it; and I was obliged to write an account

count of it to the King so plainly and impartially, that all the Prince's complaints on his side were infignificant; which, added to his jealoufy of the Court, incited him to command away all the land-forces to *Yarmouth*; where they lay incamped all summer by the fea-fide, without being ever reimbarked, or able to do the leaft fervice. Monfieur DE SCHOMBERG obeyed, but took no leave of the Prince, and ingaged me prefently to carry him a challenge after the expedition was over; which the King prevented, tho' not out of kindnefs to either of them: For as he was unfatisfied with the Prince's conduct that fummer, fo Monfieur DE SCHOMBERG's popularity, among the difaffected gentlemen in the country, was unjuftly reprefented to his prejudice by fome Papifts there, who took his affable fort of behaviour (which he thought neceffary in a ftranger, intending to fettle here) for a factious defign of complying with the country Party.

THIS was the caufe of the Duke of MONMOUTH's advancement; for the Duke of YORK, efteeming his forwardnefs and inclination to the war, thought him the fitteft perfon to be fet up againft SCHOMBERG,

from

from whom he was now perfectly alienated; and so made his court to the King at the same time by recommending his beloved Son to be at the head of our military affairs, which himself hoped to influence still by that means. Yet SCHOMBERG's staying here, to which he was inclined by his disposition as well as religion, had been an invincible obstacle to all these designs; if the disgust he took at being refused the Garter, had not soon contributed to his leaving us; which favour it seems he had long desired, tho' so privately, that I happened to receive the promise of it in his camp at *Tarmouth*, without having the least imagination that my General had been my rival; who resented it a little the more, because it was then bestowed on one who was but a Colonel under him. Thus all things concurr'd with the Duke of MONMOUTH's ambition, as soon as Prince RUPERT was out of favour, and the Duke of YORK out of capacity, by reason of the late Test against *Papists*.

THERE was yet one thing more, which in exactness I must not omit, that much contributed to this young man's advancement; I mean the great friendship which the Duke of YORK had openly professed to his Wife,

I   a

a lady of wit, and reputation; who had both the ambition of making her husband confiderable, and the addrefs of fucceeding in it, by ufing her intereft in fo friendly an Uncle, whofe defign I believe was only to convert her. Whether this familiarity of theirs was contrived, or only connived at by the Duke of MONMOUTH himfelf, is hard to determine: But I well remember that after thefe two Princes had become declared enemies, the Duke of YORK one day told me with fome emotion, as conceiving it a new mark of his nephew's infolence, that he had forbidden his wife to receive any more vifits from him. At which I could not forbear frankly replying, that I who was not ufed to excufe him, yet could not hold from doing it in that cafe; wifhing his Highnefs might have no jufter caufe to complain of him. Upon which the Duke, furprized to find me excufe his and my own enemy, changed the difcourfe immediately.

THE firft ftep of the Duke of MONMOUTH's rifing to authority in the army, was his being intrufted with the care, tho' not the command of it; which the Lord ARLINGTON confented to (notwithftanding in *France*, 'tis a part of his province, as chief Secretary

tary of State) both in friendfhip to him', and for his own eafe, fince it faved him the trouble of fuch affairs, without diminution either to his power or profit; fince all com-miffions ftill paffed through the Secretary's hands, and only orders now through the Duke's. The fecond advance he made, was the King's fending his commands to every Colonel that they fhould obey all directions which came from the Duke of MONMOUTH. This wanted but the formality of a com-miffion to make him an abfolute General; and yet even thus far the Duke of YORK af-fifted him, fo blinded he was by his fond-nefs of either husband or wife, or rather I think of both together.

BUT now an odd accident, only worth relating on that account, will let us fee the great uncertainty of court affairs, as well as the ignorance of thofe who moft commonly write of them; very gravely attributing to prudence, or providence, what is often no-thing elfe but humour, love, or jealoufy: For, notwithftanding all this intimacy be-tween the Duke of YORK, and his Nephew; fuch a firm one, that even a direct contrary intereft was unable to weaken; yet a little inconftancy in one of their Miftreffes, tho'

in favour of a third perſon, was the acci-
dental cauſe of ſuch a diviſion between them,
as never ceas'd till it coſt one of them the
hazard of his Crown, and the other that of
his Life on a Scaffold.

ALL which, in compliance with your
commands, ſhall be ſet down freely and faithfully, tho' not poſſible to be recounted without too frequent mention of my ſelf.

AT our return from *Tarmouth*, the old
Holland regiment was given me, and joined
to another I had raiſed ; by which I remain'd in command after the peace, when
all our new Colonels were disbanded. This,
I ſuppoſe, made thoſe two Dukes think of
me ſoon after for commanding the firſt regiment of Foot-guards, and deſign'd the King
ſhould buy Colonel RUSSEL out of it for
that purpoſe ; having before prevailed with
the good Lord CRAVEN to let me come
over his head, who commanded the ſecond
regiment. But juſt while this was ſettling,
the Duke of MONMOUTH, ever ingaged
in ſome Amour, falls into great Anger
againſt me, for an unlucky diſcovery that
made too much noiſe in the Court at that
time.

VOL. II.   D   HE

HE had always great temper, and therefore offered no affront on the place; but wanted not the cunning to revenge himself a better way, by privately obtaining a promise of the King to let him have that command which was defigned for me : forefeeing then his own would become void, and perhaps be given to me, he propofed the Earl of OSSORY for that, againft whom there could be no objection; fo ftopping up my way in both places.

THE Duke of YORK having openly made us friends, fufpected no fuch artifice and counterplotting in his Nephew as he found him but too capable of afterwards, in a much greater matter : Accordingly he thought it time to move the King about that alteration in the Guards, not in the leaft apprehending a repulfe. For the King, tho' of more Wit than moft of thofe who influenced him, had that *Foible* of his Family to be eafily impofed on; fo that it was a conftant method among his Minifters, firft to fettle what they agreed to be done, and then offer it to the King; like an Act of Parliament, to which the negative voice is feldom apprehended.

BUT

BUT now that way of proceeding was the loss of our business, and the design miscarried only by the closeness of its management: For, the King assured his Brother, that never dreaming of this his proposal he was ingaged already, but yet to another of his great friends; and then naming him, wondred at his being no sooner acquainted with it.

THE Duke was pleased to tell me this presently with great resentment, not only for my disappointment, but that an alteration should be resolved on in the two best commands of the army, without his being first acquainted with it. It was natural for a man who lost his pretension, not to lessen this concern in the Duke; and therefore I, who during the Duke of MONMOUTH's quarrel to me, had often tried in vain to shake his interest in that Prince, would not lose so fair an occasion to part them for ever.

I told him therefore of how little importance my own share in this business was, which I found amply recompensed by his being so much concerned about it. But I confess'd my self extreamly troubled at

another

another part of this affair, which gave me
a ſtrange ſort of ſuſpicion. The Duke
could not fail to inquire what it was, and
with a ſeeming reluctance I explained it.
That the Duke of MONMOUTH's own command of the horſe life-guard, was better
than Colonel RUSSEL's regiment of foot,
both for honour and profit; and therefore
he would hardly change it thus, without
ſome ill deſign, to which twenty four com-
panies of foot might be more uſeful, than
a ſingle troop of horſe.

THAT, diſappointing of me, was not
his only aim; ſince he might have had that
ſatisfaction as well by getting the Earl of
OSSORY into that regiment, without taking
it himſelf by leaving a better poſt for it.

As the Duke grew warm at this, I ingag'd him more, by freely quitting my own
pretenſion, if his Highneſs could find a truſty
man for it, whom the Duke of MONMOUTH
could have no pretence to oppoſe, as he
did me, on account of our quarrel; repre-
ſenting it to be a poſt of ſuch conſequence,
that, one day, perhaps, no leſs a thing than
the Crown of *England* might depend on
it.

THE

THE Duke accepted kindly the laying down my pretenfion, and propofed fome others for that command, but to no purpofe: For, the King reproach'd him with oppofing a thing already fettled between Himfelf and his Son. Upon which almoft in defpair, he tried a little with my Lord ARLINGTON, the Duke of MONMOUTH's great Advifer at that time; freely making him underftand, That if the Duke of MONMOUTH would not defift of himfelf from preffing it any farther, he muft lofe his friendfhip, which had been fo ufeful to him; and confequently, pay too dear a price for what was but a trifle in comparifon with it: To which, that dextrous Minifter replied fomething haughtily, That the Duke of MONMOUTH could not need his favour more than his Highnefs needed the King's, which he might hazard to leffen, by thus croffing his inclinations for fo beloved a Son.

WITH this furprifing anfwer from a Secretary of State, the Duke grew more concern'd than ever; and at laft was driven on the only expedient now left; which, in the firft place, ferv'd the Duke's intereft by fecuring

curing

curing that employment in safe hands; and, next, my own revenge, in keeping the Duke of MONMOUTH out of it. He was advised therefore to send immediately for Colone RUSSEL, who was very covetous, and by any means whatsoever, *viz.* by any money, to charm him out of his resolution to sell his command; which the King was so far from imposing on an ancient officer of such merit and quality, that he kindly assur'd him, no such change had ever been thought of, if Mr. RUSSEL himself had not ask'd the favour of selling his command, for the good of his Heir. What passed between the Duke and RUSSEL, is not hard to guess; for, the latter kept his command by pretending to the King, that, when it came to the point, he could not find in his heart to quit his service, and desired to die in it : But upon all this matter followed such an animosity between those two Princes, as will serve to fill our Annals with the fatal effects of it, while yet this first occasion of their breach is not like to be so much as mentioned.

THE Turns of Court are such, that, after all this bustle and composition between us about this regiment of Guards; a third person

son not then thought of for such a command, nor so much as in the army, luckily got it from us both by the Duke of YORK'S being absent in *Scotland*, and RUSSEL's quitting his interest, on account of the Popish Plot; and so renewing his desire to sell. The Duke of MONMOUTH at that time was in such disfavour, as to have his Government of *Hull* and Lord-Lieutenancy of *Yorkshire* given to me; which, with the old *Holland* regiment I had before, was already more than, being so young, I could reasonably pretend to. The King therefore, at last, bought that command of Colonel RUSSEL for his other Son the Duke of GRAFTON. What appears in this Story most remarkable, is the probability that in those early days the Duke of MONMOUTH had some thoughts of what he attempted afterward; and the suspicion of him thus accidentally infused into the Duke of YORK, was not without some ground: Since that regiment consisted of Two thousand four hundred men, a great part of our little army, always kept together; and quartered in *London,* when the other few regiments were separated into all the Garrisons of *England*.

THIS

THIS appear'd fufficiently at King CHARLES's
death, when it had not been impoffible for
the Duke of MONMOUTH to fucceed him, if
he had then flourifhed in Court at the head
of fo confiderable a regiment.

THE

THE
CHARACTER
OF A
TORY,

In ANSWER to That of a
TRIMMER:

Both written in King CHARLES's Reign.

THE

PREFACE.

I SHALL begin my PREFACE with a Paradox, and assure the reader most solemnly, That neither favour nor faction, interest nor vanity, neither the design of helping my friends, or of hurting my enemies, have had the least share in this small undertaking, and (which I confess is scarce credible in so corrupt an age) that nothing under heaven but the publick good had been able to have tempted me to expose my quiet, and perhaps my reputation, among a crowd of such impertinent scriblers as at this time swarm among us. But it being a little unreasonable for me to expect your belief of so unusual a sincerity, only on the bare word of a stranger; 'tis necessary

by

by that which follows, to convince my im-
partial reader, that I was really moved by
this honest design ; because there could be
indeed no other temptation to undertake it.
For I am extreamly sensible that the book
I am about to answer is written not only on
a very plausible subject, but with all man-
ner of advantage and eloquence ; and not
an eloquence only full of fallacious colours,
that fall off as soon as brought to the light
of a strict examination ; but of as good and
solid reasons as that cause will bear ; a cause
too that must be acknowledged not unwor-
thy of so able an advocate : For what is
more self-denying and meritorious, than to
disoblige both parties of WHIG *and* TORY,
in order only to maintain the disinterested
name of TRIMMER? *What is more prudent*
than to avoid those enticing partialities on
either hand, by steering so right in the mid-
dle, unprevailed on by the strongest temp-
tations? What is more vertuous and noble,
than to keep out of all extreams, and to
remain in that golden mean where alone they
say vertue is always to be found? I should
still go on in our TRIMMER's *praise, if I*
were

were not afraid of being thought a flatterer; and that perhaps the reader might compare us to our late noble duellists, who instead of engaging heartily, agreed to set up for heroes, by giving each other a few slight hurts, and a world of commendations. Besides this, I am but too sensible of a greater disadvantage, which lies in the mighty difference there is between writing first on any subject, and answering what is already written; the thought of invention in the writer, and the novelty of it to the reader, are such great advantages on one side, that more than ordinary skill is necessary on the other, to keep up the combat with any tolerable reputation. But I am comforted and armed against all these disencouragements, by the great value I have for my adversary, by whom it were no shame to be worsted, and by my cause, for which I should think it some glory to suffer, out of my too much zeal to maintain it: And though I call him my adversary, 'tis by custom, and for distinction sake, since I doubt not but we both contend alike for truth, and for the benefit of our dearest country; and therefore, surely, have no more reason

reaſon to be angry with one another, than any two adventurers who ſearch for the ſame treaſure, tho' in different mines, and by different methods.

The

The Character of a TORY, &c. in 1679. In Answer to That of a TRIMMER, and written at the same Time, but never printed.

IN the first place I must lay down one necessary Observation to be remembred throughout this whole discourse, that a multitude of wise and vertuous sayings are so intermixed with our TRIMMER's particular
ticular

ticular opinions, that it is indeed the principal part of my work only to diſtinguiſh thoſe uncontroverted points from the reſt. And I cannot imagine why ſuch plain undeniable truths are aſſerted with ſo much eloquence, unleſs in them to wrap up the more dangerous opinions, which otherwiſe could hardly be ſwallowed by any unprejudiced reader. I confeſs I ſo much reverence his good reaſoning ſometimes, that I cannot but grieve at his bad; and am aſtoniſh'd to find the ſame man capable of ſo unequal a mixture: yet after all, ſuch is human nature at the beſt, and who alas can help it? We were not men but angels, if we always thought as wiſely as this TRIMMER does ſometimes; but I muſt have leave alſo to ſay, we ſhould be ſcarcely reaſonable creatures, if ſuch groſs errors as his are, could be capable of deceiving us: however the very good reflections that he makes ſometimes, deſerve excuſe for his bad ones; which alſo at the ſame time they are condemned, yet claim methinks a kind of reſpect due to ſuch illuſtrious criminals.

To begin the trial, I join iſſue with him in believing it a fault of government, when they at the bar ſeem to dictate laws, that is, is, domineer over thofe on the bench; but fure 'tis not fo great a proof of learning in the lawyer, and of ignorance in the judge, as of arrogance in the one and remiffnefs in the other. Nor can I fee why a criminal's own proteftation of his innocence, may not be as good an argument at any time to prove it, and perfuade the people to believe it, as the reputation of his advocate, tho' never fo learned, who is bound to plead for him or any body elfe that gives him a fee. Sure, neither the perfon accufed, nor he that pleads for him, can in reafon be fo credible in their own cafe, as the Twelve Judges, whom the wife always fubmit to, if they are able ones, in reafon; and if they are ignorant, in prudence; becaufe in all matters whatfoever, there muft be fome perfons refer'd to on both fides, without appeal to the People; who, tho' perhaps in other matters, as trade, &c. they feldom miftake their intereft, yet can never be fuppofed impartial and judicious in cafes of this kind: Therefore my Lord BACON obferves well, That in a Judge, popularity is a greater fault than bribery; becaufe every body is capable of flattery, but few of making prefents. So that all which the TRIMMER fo enlarges on,

amounts to no more than this, That 'tis better for a nation to have honeſt and learned
judges, than ignorant and corrupt ones ;
and what TORY denies it ? Only in this the
TORY is, ſure, the more reaſonable, that
tho' he would never adviſe his Prince to
chooſe ill men for judges, he would as little
put the people on diſliking them when once
choſen, and would attribute ſuch a miſcar-
riage or rather misfortune only to his Prince's
not being omniſcient, and conſequently capable of being miſinformed or impoſed on.
Now, methinks, this is more conſiſtent with
what our TRIMMER ſays afterwards, than he
is with himſelf ; for certainly the way to
ſuch a happy ſettlement between King and
People, as that one of them ſhould be almoſt ready to adore the other, is not to
quarrel with his proceedings, but rather to
excuſe them, tho' never ſo faulty ; for tho'
our TRIMMER is ſo zealous a Courtier, as
he would have his King admired like a
God, I ſuppoſe he does not expect he ſhould
really be one, that is, free from all manner
of frailties.

WHAT our TRIMMER ſays about Armies
is unanſwerable, when they are employ-
ed not for defence of the Government,
but

but either to set up a false title, or oppress the subjects under a good one. But there is a meaning in this case, and for all the TRIMMER's pretence to moderation, the understanding TORY only shews it, who would have soldiers enough to protect the Government, but not to invade it : and therefore our army in *England* (tho' perhaps our great officers may not approve it, and 'tis no matter, since their advice in State-matters is not like to be asked) augmented as it is, and well disciplined as it ought to be, is but an assistance to the *Posse-Comitatus*, and a General, in effect, does but obey a Constable. Upon this ground I dare conclude, that a competent force in defence of the King's person and prerogative, is as necessary a support to the Government, as the Law-courts are in *Westminster-hall :* But who can help it if the TRIMMER's eyes are so daz'led with the glittering of a little army on *Putney-heath*, and his ears so stunn'd with trumpets and kettle-drums, that he has quite forgotten the opposition that has been made these last fifty years, to the undoubted right of the Crown, and consequently to the peace of the Nation. Let him but think well of the factious and republican principles among

us,

us, and of the unparallell'd boldneſs our nation always ſhews in the worſt deſigns as
well as the beſt ; and my good opinion of
our TRIMMER gives me almoſt an aſſurance,
that he will conclude ten thouſand ſoldiers
are now as neceſſary to the King's ſafety,
and the people's quiet, as ever the band of
penſioners and yeomen of the guard were
heretofore.   And I am confident he will
believe that, as in times of great oppreſſion
and injuſtice, it would not be indecent for
the *Houſe of Commons* to deſire moderate
laws for their future preſervation againſt it,
and that they ought not for that to be ſuſpected of rebellion ; ſo when the ballance is
too much on the other ſide, and Kings only
are in the danger, 'tis ſure at leaſt as fitting
and as reaſonable for them to encreaſe their
guards and ſtrength, which ought not to
breed the leaſt ſuſpicion in their ſubjects.
So that 'tis not the uſe, but ill uſe of Armies
that can be reaſonably complained of ; and
the TRIMMER is forced to confeſs, the beſt
things are ſubject to that ſometimes ; ſince
he cannot deny that misfortune to have happened even in Parliaments themſelves.

I am entirely of the TRIMMER's opinion
as to printing of Books only on one ſide,
and

and think it a very naufeous partiality; and for that very reafon I approve of the publifhing thofe on the Crown's part at prefent, to counterpoife the much greater number written of late on the people's, till at laft fuch a happy fettlement may follow, that it will be, I hope, as prepofterous to write a book in defence of loyalty, as of rebellion; no man in the world doubting the one, or endeavouring the other. 'Tis true, indeed, that perpetually cramming down peoples throats even the beft diet, is enough to make their ftomachs rife againft it; but I hope the TRIMMER will not propofe a thing fo partial, as to let all the libels remain unanfwered, though I confefs, moft of them deferve to be fo.

I am alfo as much as the TRIMMER againft dividing the Sovereignty with any the neareft Kindred, much lefs with Affemblies; but think neither *England* nor *Mufcovy* good inftances of its inconvenience, which yet muft be attributed only to our good fortune; and that being nothing but fome lefs obferved caufe, I will endeavour to inform the reader as to *England*; and leave the famous pen of Sir PETER WYCHE to do as much for *Mufcovy*.

E 3

IT

IT has fo happen'd here, that the only Brother and Heir of the Crown is a Prince indefatigable both in peace and war, and a zealous induftrious Minifter of State : This draws, as one may well imagine, a multitude of dependers after him, and in another Subject would have been counted a meritorious fervice to his King and Country ; but in one fo nearly related to the Crown, is fufpected of ambition and defign, by fome of thofe who judge at a diftance. But I refer the TRIMMER and my felf to all thofe who approach him nearer, if ever there was a conduct more difinterefted, more humble, or more fubmiffively obedient ; which I confefs is fo extraordinary a thing, that I cannot blame the TRIMMER for fo prudent a precaution, it not being a Politician's bufinefs to depend on Miracles.

I concur intirely in believing it hardly poffible that any foreign dangers fhould be too fudden for a Parliament's affembling ; but fure 'tis not impoffible for affemblies to be factious and dilatory, even bribed to be fo, by that very power which produces the danger ? What if this fhould happen ? Why, the TRIMMER himfelf cannot but admit of the remedy ; (and to fhew my compliance

in

in requital of his) he cannot more approve the thing, than I do his silence concerning it. For 'tis a *Sanctum Sanctorum* to be approach'd but seldom even by Princes, and then too with fear and reverence. I agree also with the TRIMMER as to Parliaments in general, and think no King of *England,* without their concurrence, can be either great abroad, or absolute at home ; and so I have done with his opinions about Laws and Government : My next work is to consider what he says of Religion.

AND here I must give that due applause which our TRIMMER deserves, since nothing can be more reasonable, more good-natured and moral, than all his reflections on the *Roman Catholicks* and the late pretended Plot, which he says ought no more to involve the whole party, tho' it were real, than the Gunpowder-treason did before ; because if the crimes of particular men, were chargeable on all those who profess the same principles, what might not *Atheists* and *Infidels* object against Christianity it self, there being no sect in it free in all its members from most horrid impieties. I doubt not but our TRIMMER's so laudable moderation in this particular, has already found its re-

E 4

ward

ward in that great satisfaction which being in the right most commonly brings along with it ; for, before this time, he cannot but with all the world be convinced of the innocence even of the most suspected *Catholicks* : how necessary then was his caution, not to prosecute all the rest for their sakes ! But as he goes on in deploring the hard condition of them, and other dissenters ; as if there was no remedy but patience for the unreasonable severity of laws, 'till a Parliament thought fit to repeal them, tho' every man alive should groan under the oppression : sure the TORY in this appears the more prudent, who can find a happy expedient in that essential necessary power belonging to all sorts of Government, for granting any temporary dispensation from penalties too hard to be inflicted, and too heavy to be endured.

AND when we consider how the very law of nature allows, nay, obliges us in some extraordinary exigents, to kill another, rather than suffer some sort of oppression and violence ; and that consequently every man in such cases hath a dispensing power within himself to break the law, deserving rather reward than punishment for so doing :

Who

Who then can doubt that Government should be so deficient, as to want a Power of preserving it self, which 'tis against nature for any private man to be without; and if this is requisite in some cases, who is so fit to judge of those as the supreme Magistrate, entrusted with the whole executive power of a nation? For, to join assemblies with him in this, tho' I approve it in his legislative capacity, is the same as to exclude all power of dispensing in any case whatsoever; since it supposes only such as cannot admit of due time for the slow deliberation of assemblies; or when those assemblies are too much possess'd with passion or prejudice.

I agree, and am glad whenever I can do so, with his despising the assistance of a drunken club, tho' made so by no other health than the King's, and I think such a mixture of affectation and disorder deserves rather a constable's staff, for its dispersing and punishment, than a blue ribband or a great title for its countenance. But I cannot think a Pulpit as insignificant as a Tavern, unless I saw one of such a club get into it; because I know no reason so good for the appointing preachers once a week to entertain the people, as the teaching them morality,

lity, a principal part of which is obedience to magiſtrates.

AFTER this, our TRIMMER obſerves that 'tis a little partial to conſider *Catholicks* always as good ſubjects, and other diſſenters as bad ones; when we may remember each of them has had their turn of being ſometimes loyal, and ſometimes rebellious. Now I am afraid, our very TRIMMER himſelf is ſomething partial; for tho' I am far from believing *Papiſts*, or any ſort of people whatſoever, ſo perfect as to be incapable of ill deſigns; yet I muſt needs obſerve with all the world, that of late years, and within this nation (which ſure are the moſt conſiderable precedents to us) *Roman Catholicks* have been all moſt remarkably loyal; and I wiſh I could ſay as much for all other diſſenters. But there is little need of defending the *Catholicks* any longer againſt our TRIMMER, who has ſaid more for them, than ever they did for themſelves; in ſhewing us how plainly 'tis their intereſt, as much as any other mens whatſoever, to ſupport this Government and defend it from all uſurpations even of *Rome* it ſelf, if ever it ſhould attempt any; and I think when intereſt ties men to obedience, 'tis a very unreaſ reasonable jealousy to suspect them. But I will now pass with the TRIMMER to things abroad, and agree with him in thinking it a very melancholy prospect.

I am sensible, even to an anxiety of mind, of our giving all the advantage imaginable to the enemies of the *English* nation abroad, by our perpetual disagreement at home ; and (according to the *Scotch* manner of proceeding against criminals) I conclude with him first as to the crime, which I think horrid beyond a name, and then afterwards examine calmly who is the unexcusable criminal : In order to which inquisition, I must truly and impartially state the case. A King and Parliament are disagreeing upon mutual jealousies ; the King apprehends any opposition to *France*, for fear the Parliament should either not supply him sufficiently to maintain it, or else take that advantage of exacting too much from the Crown. On the other side the Parliaments are hearty towards such an opposition, because 'tis the nation's interest, and are sufficiently resolved to maintain it ; but at the same time are afraid of the King's employing their supplies another way. Now as I cannot deny but 'tis the *French* King's interest to tempt Him any way, if it were possible,

possible, and to increase his suspicion of Parliaments; so the TRIMMER also must needs
own, that the same foreign Power is as
busy in the House of Commons, to widen
the breach on that side too: and thus is a
mighty Monarch with both hands tearing
us silently in pieces, and widening those
very wounds, which we have first given our
selves. But is it fair? is it just? is it impartial (as a TRIMMER pretends to be) to impute all these inconveniencies to the Court
alone, who are no more capable of helping
it, without a Parliament's compliance; than
the Parliament is, without the King's con-
descension in maintaining the *English* interest against the *French*, at their so earnest
desires? But since things must needs con-
tinue thus, 'till one side a little submits, is
it hard to determine which should first yield;
the Children, or the Father? the Subjects,
or the Sovereign? the Parliament, or the
King?

I hope our TRIMMER's veneration for his
country is no idolatry, for I cannot hold
from kneeling down by him, and kissing
our mother Earth with all the tenderness
imaginable, for which I have a good sub-
stantial reason, as plain as the Clown who
taught

taught it me; and that is, becaufe I have
my livelihood here, and thefe foreign tref-
paffers would be apt to take it from me; fo
that I too, without pretending to be a Hero,
would rather die generoufly in defence of
my Country, than ftarve infamoufly after
the lofs of it.   Therefore, whenever the
Trimmer can perfuade the Parliament to
give money enough for a Fleet againft *France*,
the Tory will engage to go a voluntier in
it, rather than command the *Kitchin Tatcht*
to any grand Louis of them all: fo I hope
we are agreed as to that point.   But whereas
our Trimmer infinuates a little artificially,
that our fettlement at home is flighted only
in order to affift the *French* defigns abroad;
I muft confefs that our divifions on this fide
of the fea, contribute fufficiently to thofe
on the other; but who can help it? 'Tis
certain, thefe two misfortunes go together;
and *England* cannot be embroil'd, without
Flanders being almoft conquered; but is
this divifion here the effect, or rather the
caufe of that Monarch's ambition? To fay
'tis the effect, is fo fharp a cenfure on our
nation, that I dare not be fo bold as our
Trimmer is, only to hint at it; and my
blood rifes at the very thought: But this I
dare

2

dare fay, becaufe 'tis manifeft, that if the ambition of *France* has caufed our diforders ; a Kingdom cannot be fo betrayed, unlefs its King be fo too. Which of his fubjects ought moft to be fufpected in fuch a cafe, I will not determine ; but whoever they are, may they be thrown out, like JONAS, to allay the ftorm, and be forced to feek a fhelter with that great Leviathan. The TORY is content, nay defirous to fearch every corner, even of the Court it felf, where fure he cannot long be hid, becaufe the Prince is a thoufand times more concern'd to find him out, than any of his moft fufpicious fubjects can be : but pray let us have fair play to fearch other places too, and not believe this *French* Monarch fo extravagantly afpiring, as to fcorn the bribing any body below a Minifter of State ; he is very well bred ; and we know his condefcenfion fuch, that the meaneft member of the *Houfe of Commons* need not defpair of being acceptable in his fight.

THE conclufion of our TRIMMER's difcourfe is very properly called fo, becaufe it feems impoffible to carry a fallacy further, or difguife it better ; and therefore I hope it will not put him out of his fo much boaft-
ed

ed moderation, if I ftrip it of all thofe artificial colours, and expofe it to the World in its mifhapen nakednefs : Then we fhall quickly fee the difference between the homelinefs of Error, and that amiable Truth fo much celebrated by our TRIMMER, who alas miftakes deformity for her, and feems in his rapture as extravagantly doting as the humorous Lieutenant, when he took his old King for a plump girl of fifteen.

WHAT do men ail, cries our TRIMMER, thus to rail at moderation, and to fay TRIMMERS are even worfe than rebels? It looks, fays he, as if they were aiming at fome violent extream, incompatible with all difcretion and moderation. This now has an appearance of reafon, and feems fair at a diftance ; but, well confider'd, is but a cloud of fallacy, without any fubftantial force of argument. Suppofe a father or mafter finds himfelf opprefs'd by any fort of ill ufage, and accordingly implores the help of his children or fervants, who yet all the while ftand carelefs by with a moft provoking indifference, rather feeming to infult over his need of their affiftance, than eager to relieve him by it : They, ftill unconcerned, behold their parent or mafter ftruggling with his adver-

faries,

faries, and extreamly fuffering either by fuits of Law or perfonal Violence, or by any other way you can fuppofe a man abufed: The good man himfelf, nay, all the world, accufes thefe luke-warm friends, thofe infamous fervants, thefe unnatural children, of being fo fhamefully unconcerned in all thefe quarrels. May not they as well anfwer for themfelves, what does this man ail? What does the world mean to find fault with our moderation, is it not a vertue? is it not a fign of fenfe as well as juftice to be ever impartial? Let us leave this parent, this mafter to his own ftrength, and let that help him out of all his troubles: why fhould we take part on either fide? O but then the good man is enraged more againft them than all his enemies. And can we blame him? what can they fay for themfelves? Why only this; Is he driving, fay they, at any ftrange extream? does he defign to beggar all his neighbours, to affault his acquaintance, to abufe all the world, that he expects we fhould affift him on all occafions?

Now let any man judge if this be a laudable moderation in thefe cold friends? A bleffed ferene temper above the clouds of paffion and partiality? Or rather, an un-worthy

worthy and unnatural coldnefs, for thofe whom they ought to be inclined to believe in the right, and to protect, tho' never fo much in the wrong ? Suppofe the quarrel began on our parents fide ; fuppofe he was contentious ; (which is laying the objection as hard as can be) yet are we at liberty either to help or hurt him, as our fancy leads us ? Are we not tied to his affiftance more firmly than foldiers are to their General by a little pay ; and not to examine the caufe fo much as the kindred ; fince our reafon and our reverence ought to conclude the beft of fuch things which we cannot be able to judge of, fo well, as he whom God and Nature have fet over us ?

ANOTHER Fallacy is endeavoured to be put on us, by fhewing the great limitation a King lies under, and the extraordinary leffening of his authority, when once it engages for one party of his people, towards the deftruction of another ; which our TRIMMER calls, fhrinking from a great Monarch, into the Head of a Faction ; and therefore he is extreamly troubled for fuch a diminution of his Prince's power. Now I confefs, this appears to me juft as if a highway-man, overtaken by a hue and cry, fhould ftand at bay, and thus pretend to wheedle the pursuing constable. What! will you, reverend Magistrates! (for 'tis time to give good words) who are entrusted by the nation with the publick peace and tranquillity, and therefore not only strengthened with ample power, but adorned with awful staffs of authority: What! will you be thus partial to these witnesses, to these shabby fellows who pretend to be robbed, as to fall on us who never saw your faces before? This is making your selves the Heads of a pursuing rabble, who one day perhaps may be indited of a riot for so abusing us - - - - - - I need not apply the comparison, because the thing speaks it self.   And whereas our TRIMMER blames people for so monopolizing a Prince's favour, that a poor TRIMMER can get none of it; I confess 'tis true, but methinks not very strange. I allow his Simile to hold good, that not only these Statesmen, but any other men in the world, even TRIMMERS themselves, would engross the very sunshine, with the hazard of being burnt, in case there were not enough of it for every body? And, for my part, tho' 'tis a great fault in mankind, I cannot but charitably forgive it; because I am one of that race

my

my felf; and bad is the beft of us all, WHIG, TORY, and TRIMMER.

BUT here he advifes us extreamly well, not to opprefs the people, which, tho' a dull heavy beaft, may yet at laft be enraged with fuch burning cupping-glaffes. In return to his kindnefs I will put him alfo in mind, that 'tis every whit as dangerous to wake a fleeping Lion; it being a great deal better to feed quietly by him than infolently tread on him, or fo much as feem to flight him : For, tho' 'tis eafier for himfelf as well as others to lock up his claws, and lie in quiet; yet if too much difturbed, perhaps he may grow peevifh, and think it better once for all to rouze up his anger to purpofe, than to be fretted and provoked perpetually.

AND now, becaufe the very name of a TORY has been given to intimate a mixture of ignorance and barbarity; it will not be unneceffary to give a fhort account of his opinions, that are fuppofed to be fuch terrible bugbears; though indeed they can frighten none but very children in politicks. Firft, As to Religion, he does not believe it a meer engine of Government, invented only by the fear of fools, and improved fince by

F 2   the

the wifdom of Magiftrates ; but yet he thinks it not below the divineft Laws, to fecond or rather fanctify thofe made by our fuperiors ; and he can never imagine any Religion likely to bring us to heaven, which hinders us from living peaceably and contentedly on earth.   So that if principles of obedience to government be not the fure mark of a good religion (becaufe then MAHOMET's might pafs as well as another) yet any that makes a difturbance is to be counted a bad one, and not fit to be fuffered in a community of reafonable creatures.

A N D though he is thought fuch a Bigot of Monarchy, 'tis only where its long fettlement among us gives it a juft title to our defence, and veneration : But all this while he thinks a fubject of *Venice* would be as guilty in fhaking that auguft fabrick of Ariftocracy, as any of our Innovators can be here ; becaufe the reafon is the fame, and the general quiet as much difturbed.   He thinks obedience to Kings, as to Parents, a moral, nay, a divine law ; and that we are tied to obferve it as much by our intereft, as our duty ; and that in this, as in all other actions of morality, the publick convenience, in which our own is comprehended, ought

to

to be thought the basis of the strictest obligation. Let not therefore any body imagine the TORY so partial or so blind, as not to see faults in his superiors, because he only sighs in silence, and is rather ashamed than angry at it. For he thinks that taking publick notice of it is as ill-bred and unwise, as a man's telling his own wife of her being painted in the Drawing-room; which is not so likely to persuade her out of that fault, as to provoke her into another of a more dangerous nature. Nay, the TORY thinks sometimes the Prerogative it self too much exalted, and is afraid of its breaking with being stretch'd too high, as instruments are in danger under unskilful hands. But even in such a case, when Liberty is like the keeper's daughter at the *Tower*, fallen under the Lion's paw; 'tis prudence to have patience, and nothing can so endanger her as to attempt her rescue. No doubt but there are evils in all governments; but the lesser ones of being unwisely governed, are a thousand times to be preferred to those of Anarchy and a Civil War. Then as to foreign affairs, the TORY is as zealous as any body for the honour of his nation; and thinks the quiet of it, especially for the future,

ture, depends on our maintaining that ho_nour generously, tho' with a little seeming inconvenience. But as the TORY would be loth to see his Prince engaged in amity with any enemies to his country, since then they must be his too, whatever they may pretend to the contrary: so he would not have a Parliament so positive, though never so much in the right, as to grow imposers instead of counsellors. A King ought to be persuaded sometimes, but never violently press'd to any thing; for, besides that 'tis the way to give a disgust to the best diet, if it be cramm'd down with violence; by such an importunity, the grace of willingness is lost, which is the very life and soul of all compliances: and the Nation will rather despise, than applaud a Prince, who only yields to their desires out of too much easiness of nature. Yet after all, perhaps the honest TORY is more concern'd than any, to have his Prince always understand his interest aright; when others are glad (it may be) of his mistakes, that turn so much to his disadvantage.

AND now to shake hands and be friends, after all our disputes; I join heartily with our TRIMMER in adoring Truth, wherever I find her; who, I am confident, has been

our

our common miſtreſs all this while, and may her favour only decide the quarrel: If ſhe were to be flattered into kindneſs, I muſt certainly ſubmit to my rival, who ſays the fineſt things of her in the world ; but ſhe is too plain her ſelf, to be delighted with compliments ; and one fair argument will gain her better than a thouſand flouriſhes. Therefore tho' I might entertain my ſelf with as many reflections as he does ; That our Climate is a TRIMMER as to its air, perpetually cloudy, low'ring, and uncertain ; That our Church too, with reverence be it ſpoken, is in this a TRIMMER, wanting enthuſiaſm on one hand, which is the only pretence for ſeparation, and yet without any ſuch authority on the other, whereby to blind men to obey her ; That our Laws alſo are errant TRIMMERS, ſparing no body that ſtands in their way, let them be of what principle they pleaſe. But here I am quite out of breath, and can go no further with our TRIMMER, ſince nothing leſs than Vertue and the Divinity it ſelf will ſerve him to be made TRIMMERS ; and that provokes me almoſt to make them TORIES, to be revenged on him : but I adore them too much for ſuch a profanation, and am too

F 4   much

much scandalized with the freedom he has already taken, to follow so unjustifiable an example,

I shall conclude with this, That what the TRIMMER only in words pretends to do, and fails of in effect, the TORY uses the right means for, and so accomplishes. For first, the TRIMMER complains of WHIGS weighing down the boat on one side, while he is wishing it should go more steddy; but yet without using the least means towards it, he sits still at the bottom of the vessel, and only quarrels with every body in it: Now what possible way is there in nature to set all right again, but by counterpoising that weight of WHIGS with as great an one of TORIES on the other side? This is all we aim at; that the Government at last may be well established, and every thing go so even, that nothing hereafter may endanger it.

WHEN TRIMMERS shall once see us in that condition, I am apt to think them so wise as to grow TORIES immediately; not doubting but they will join then, as heartily as any of us all, in the preservation of that happy settlement; towards which I hope we are drawing nearer every day, and in which I pray we may rest for ever.

A

A

CHARACTER

OF

CHARLES II.

King of *ENGLAND*.

A
CHARACTER
OF
CHARLES II.

I HAVE pitch'd on this Character of CHARLES II. not for his being a King, or my having had the honour to ferve him : The firft of thefe would be too vulgar a confideration, and the other too particular. But I think it a Theme of great variety, and whatever is wanting in the writer, may, I hope, be recompenfed in the agreeablenefs of the fubject; which is fometimes enough to recommend a picture though ill-drawn, and to make a face one likes, oftner look'd on, than the beft piece of RAPHAEL.

To begin then according to cuftom with his *Religion,* which fince his death hath. made fo much noife in the world ; I yet dare confidently affirm it to be only that which is vulgarly (tho' unjuftly) counted none at all, I mean *Deifm*. And this uncommon opinion he owed more to the liveliness of his parts, and carelessness of his temper, than either to reading or much confideration; for, his quickness of apprehension at first view could discern thro' the several cheats of pious pretences; and his natural laziness confirm'd him in an equal mistrust of them all, for fear he should be troubled with examining which Religion was best.

I f in his early travels, and late administration, he seem'd a little biass'd to one fort of Religion; the first is only to be imputed to a certain easiness of temper, and a complaisance for that company he was then forced to keep: and the last was no more than his being tired (which he soon was in any difficulty) with those bold oppositions in Parliament; which made him almost throw himself into the arms of a *Roman Catholick* party, so remarkable in *England* for their loyalty, who embraced him gladly, and lull'd him asleep with those enchanting songs of absolute sovereignty, which the best and wisest of Princes are often unable to resist.

A n d tho' he engaged himself on that side more fully at a time, when 'tis in vain,

and

and too late to diffemble ; we ought lefs to
wonder at it, than to confider that our very
judgments are apt to grow in time as partial as our affections : And thus by accident
only, he became of their opinion in his
weaknefs, who had fo much endeavoured
always to contribute to his power.

H E loved eafe and quiet, to which his
unneceffary wars are fo far from being a
contradiction, that they are rather a proof of
it ; fince they were made chiefly to comply
with thofe perfons, whofe diffatisfaction
would have proved more uneafy to one of
his humour, than all that diftant noife of
cannon, which he would often liften to with
a great deal of tranquillity. Befides, the
great and almoft only pleafure of mind he
appeared addicted to, was fhipping and fea-
affairs ; which feemed to be fo much his talent both for knowledge, as well as inclination, that a war of that kind was rather an
entertainment, than any difturbance to his
thoughts.

I F he did not go himfelf at the head of
fo magnificent a fleet, 'tis only to be imputed to that eagernefs of military glory in
his Brother ; who, under the fhew of a decent care for preferving the Royal Perfon

2

from

from danger, ingrofs'd all that fort of honour to himfelf; with as much jealoufy of any other's interpofing in it, as a King of another temper would have had of his, tho' without reafon; for, never Heir behaved himfelf more fubmiffively than the Duke of York, to the laft minute of his life. 'Tis certain, no Prince was ever more fitted by nature for his country's intereft than he was, in all his maritime inclinations; which might have proved of fufficient advantage to this nation, if he had been as careful in depreffing all fuch improvements in *France,* as of advancing and encouraging our own. But it feems he wanted jealoufy in all his inclinations, which leads us to confider him in his pleafures.

Where he was rather abandoned than luxurious, and like our female Libertines, apter to be debauch'd for the fatisfaction of others, than to feek with choice where moft to pleafe himfelf. I am of opinion alfo, that in his latter times there was as much of lazinefs, as of love, in all thofe hours he paffed among his miftreffes; who, after all, ferved only to fill up his *Seraglio;* while a bewitching kind of pleafure called Sauntring, and talking without any conftraint, was the true *Sultana Queen* he delighted in.   He

H E was furely inclined to Juftice, for nothing elfe would have retained him fo faft to the fucceffion of a Brother, againft a Son he was fo fond of, and the humour of a party he fo much fear'd.   I am willing alfo to impute to his juftice, whatever feems in fome meafure to contradict the general opinion of his clemency ; as his fuffering always the rigour of the Law to proceed not only againft all highway-men, but alfo feveral others ; in whofe cafes the Lawyers (according to their wonted cuftom) had ufed fometimes a great deal of hardfhip and feverity.

H I s Underftanding was quick and lively in little things, and fometimes would foar high enough in great ones ; but unable to keep it up, with any long attention or application.   Witty in all forts of converfation, and telling a ftory fo well, that not out of flattery, but for the pleafure of hearing it, we ufed to feem ignorant of what he had repeated to us ten times before, as a good comedy will bear the being feen often.

O F a wonderful mixture ; lofing all his time, and till of late, fetting his whole heart on the Fair Sex ; yet neither angry with rivals, nor in the leaft nice as to the being be-

I

beloved: and while he facrificed all things to his miftreffes, he would ufe to grudge, and be uneafy at their lofing a little of it again at play, tho' never fo neceffary for their diverfion : Nor would he venture five pounds at Tennis to thofe fervants, who might obtain as many thoufands, either before he came thither, or as foon as he left off.

N o t falfe to his word, but full of diffimulation, and very *adroit* at it ; yet no man eafier to be impofed on : for his great dexterity was in cozening himfelf, by gaining a little one way, while it coft him ten times as much another ; and by careffing thofe perfons moft, who had deluded him the oft'neft, and yet the quickeft in the world at 'fpying fuch a ridicule in another.

F a m i l i a r, eafy, and good-natur'd ; but for great offences fevere, and inflexible ; alfo in one week's abfence, quite forgetting thofe fervants, to whofe faces he could hardly deny any thing.

I n the midft of all his remiffnefs, fo induftrious and indefatigable on fome particular occafions, that no man would either toil longer, or be able to manage it better.

H e was fo liberal, as to ruin his affairs by it ; for Want in a King of *England,*
turns

turns things juft upfide down, and expofes
a Prince to his people's mercy.   It did yet
worfe in him, for it forc'd him alfo to depend on his great neighbour of *France*, who
play'd the Brother with him fufficiently, in
all thofe times of extremity ; yet this pro-
fufenefs of his did not fo much proceed from
his over-valuing thofe he favoured, as from
his under-valuing any fums of money which
he did not fee ; tho' he found his error in
this, but I confefs a little of the lateft.

H E had fo natural an averfion to all formality, that with as much wit as moft Kings
ever had, and with as majeftick a mien, yet
he could not on premeditation act the part
of a King- for a moment, either at Parliament or Council, either in words or gef-
ture ; which carried him into the other extreme, more inconvenient of the two, of
letting all diftinction and ceremony fall to
the ground as ufelefs and foppifh.

H I S temper both of Body and Mind was
admirable ; which made him an eafy generous Lover, a civil obliging Husband, a friendly Brother, an indulgent Father, and a good-
natur'd Mafter.   If he had been as follicitous
about improving the faculties of his mind,
as he was in the management of his bodily

health, tho' alas the one prov'd unable to make his life long, the other had not failed to have made it famous.

HE was an illustrious exception to all the common rules of Physiognomy; for, with a most saturnine-harsh sort of countenance, he was both of a merry and merciful dispo-sition; and in the last thirty years of his life, as fortunate, as those of his father had been dismal and tumultuous. If his death has been by some suspected of being un-timely, it may be imputed to his extreme healthy constitution; which made the world as much surpriz'd at his dying before three-score, as if nothing but an ill accident could have killed him.

I would not say any thing on so sad a subject, if I did not think silence it self would in such a case signify too much; and there-fore, as an impartial writer, I am oblig'd to observe that the most knowing and most deserving of all his physicians did not only believe him poisoned, but thought himself so too not long after, for having declared his opinion a little too boldly.

BUT here I must needs take notice of an unusual piece of Justice, which yet all the world has almost unanimously agreed in;

I mean, in not fufpecting his Succeffor of the leaft connivance in fo horrid a Villany; and perhaps there was never a more remarkable inftance of the wonderful power of Truth and Innocence. For 'tis next to a miracle, that fo unfortunate a Prince, in the midft of all thofe difadvantages he lies under, fhould be yet clear'd of this even by his greateft enemies; notwitbftanding all thofe circumftances that ufe to give a fufpicion, and that extreme malice which has of late attended him in all his other actions.

A

CHARACTER

OF THE

Earl of *Arlington.*

HENRY BENNET, a younger son
of a private gentleman, had followed
the Royal Family into exile ; at
whose restoration he was made first Privy-
Purse, then Secretary of State, Earl of AR-
LINGTON,

LINGTON, Knight of the Garter, and at laſt Lord Chamberlain to King CHARLES the Second, and to his Brother King JAMES the Second afterwards.   He was for ſome years a kind of favourite Miniſter, I mean converſant in his Maſter's pleaſures, as well as intruſted with his buſineſs ; notwithſtanding the conſtant enmity both of the Duke of YORK, and Chancellor CLARENDON, whoſe ſuperior Power, eſpecially in ſtate-affairs, was yet unable to ſhake King CHARLES's inclination to this gentleman ; who therefore, at the other's baniſhment, remained if not ſole miniſter, at leaſt the principal one for ſome time.   He met with one thing very peculiar in his fortune, which I have ſcarce known happen to any man elſe : with all his advancement (which is wont to create malice, but ſeldom contempt) he was believed in *England* by moſt people, a man of much leſs abilities than he really had.   For this unuſual ſort of miſtake I can only imagine two cauſes : Firſt, his over-cautious avoiding to ſpeak in Parliament, as having been more converſant in affairs abroad ; tho' no body performed it better

when

when oblig'd to give account of some Treaties to the *House of Lords*, or to defend himself in the *House of Commons ;* by which last he once brought himself off with great dexterity. The other reason of it I fancy to have come from the Duke of BUCKINGHAM, who being his rival in Court after the fall of CLARENDON, and having an extraordinary talent of turning any thing into ridicule, exercised it sufficiently on this Lord, both with the King and every body else : which had its effect at last even to his being left out of his Master's business, but not his favour ; which in some measure continued still, and long after this his supplanter was totally discarded.

HAVING been educated in order to be a Divine, he was a better scholar than commonly Courtiers are ; and so well versed in the *Classick Poets,* that I never knew any man apply them so properly on any subject whatsoever, and without any pedantic affectation. Yet he could never shake off a little air of formality, that an Embassy into *Spain* had infected him with ; but it only hung about his mien, without the least tincture of it either in his words or behaviour.

He

He once had the honour to procure a *Triple League* of great advantage to the defence of *Europe* againſt *France:* But he being one of thoſe who for ſeveral years afterwards aſſiſted in carrying on a quite contrary intereſt, it too plainly ſhews that, tho' none in this whole Reign knew foreign affairs ſo well, yet after all he was rather a ſubtle Courtier, than an able Stateſman ; too much regarding every inclination of his Maſter, and too little conſidering his true intereſt and that of the nation. To end handſomely with him, he was of a generous temper ; not only living ſplendidly, but obliging his friends willingly and warmly : On which occaſion I remember that, viſiting him one day, when newly a friend of his had turn'd ungratefully againſt him, he ask'd me what effect I thought it would have upon him ? I thinking he meant as to his fortune, was about to anſwer gravely ; when he ſmilingly proteſted it ſhould neither cool him in his preſent friendſhips, nor hinder his aſſiſting the next deſerving perſon who came in his way ; becauſe that was the greateſt ſatisfaction of his life, and he would not part with it upon any diſcouragement whatſoever.

The

The truth of this he told me I should always find, and indeed I did so to the very end of his life; which therefore required this small piece of gratitude.

A
LETTER
TO
Doctor *Tillotson*,

Then D E A N, afterwards

A R C H B I S H O P of *Canterbury*.

Written and Printed juſt after the Revolution.

S I R,

NOTHING in this world is, or ought to be ſo dear to any man of honour, as his reputation ; and conſequently the defence of it is the greateſt obligation that one man can lay on another. There are alſo ſome circumſtances that render this obligation yet more acceptable and valuable ; as when 'tis confer'd generouſly, without any ſelf-intereſt, or the leaſt deſire or invitation from the perſon ſo defended. All this happens to be my caſe

at

at this time; and therefore I hope you will not be furpriz'd to find I am not the moſt ungrateful and infenſible man living; which certainly I ſhould be, if I did not acknowledge all your induſtrious concern for me about the buſineſs of the Eccleſiaſtical Commiſſion, which now makes ſo much noiſe in the world. You have (as I am told) ſo cordially pleaded my cauſe, that 'tis almoſt become your own; and therefore (as unwilling as I am to ſpeak of my ſelf, eſpecially in a buſineſs which I cannot wholly excuſe) yet I think my ſelf now a little oblig'd to ſhew, that my part in this matter, though imprudent enough, yet is not altogether unworthy of ſo juſt and conſiderable an advocate.

THE leſs a man ſays for himſelf, the better; and 'tis ſo well underſtood already with what great care I was ſometimes excluded from knowing the moſt important deſigns of the Court, that I need not juſtify my ſelf, or trouble you as to thoſe matters: Only I appeal to the unqueſtionable teſtimony of the *Spaniſh* Ambaſſador, if I did not zealouſly and conſtantly take all occaſions to oppoſe the *French* intereſt; becauſe I knew it directly oppoſite both to the King and King-

Kingdom's good ; which are indeed things inseparable, and ought to be so accounted, as a fundamental maxim in all councils of Princes.

THIS I hope will prepare the way a little for what I have to say, concerning my being one of the Ecclesiastical Commissioners, of which error I am now as sensible as I was at first ignorant ; being so unhappily conversant in the midst of a perpetual Court-flattery, as never to have heard the least word of any illegality in that commission, before I was unfortunately engaged in it.

FOR though my Lord of CANTERBURY had very prudently refused to be of it ; yet it was told us at Court, and by the King himself, that his refusal proceeded only from his unwillingness to act at that time, and not from any illegality he suspected in the commission : having excus'd himself from it the most respectful way, only upon the account of his age, and the infirmities he lay under. Being thus ignorant of the Laws, and in such a station at Court and Council, I need not desire a man of your judgment and candour to consider the hardness of my case, when I was commanded to serve in a commission with a Lord Chancellor, a
Lord

Lord Chief Juſtice, and two Biſhops : **who**
had all of them acted ſome time already without ſhewing the leaſt diffidence of their
power, or any heſitation in the execution
of it. And perhaps a man of more diſcre-
tion than I can pretend to, might have been
eaſily perſuaded to act in ſuch a conjunction,
and to think he might do it ſafely, both in
Law and Conſcience. But I need not ſay
much to ſhew my deſire of avoiding, if
poſſible, a troubleſome commiſſion, that
had not the leaſt temptation of honour or
profit to recommend it ; and in which therefore you know I continued on no account
in the world, but to ſerve both the King
and Clergy with the little ability I had, in
moderating thoſe councils, which we thought
might grow higher, if I left my places to be
filled by thoſe who greedily waited for them,
in order to their fooliſh deſigns.

AND ſince I have been forced to mention
my good will at leaſt, if not my ſervice,
to ſuch learned men of the clergy, who I
thought deſerved it ; it may be allowed me
to give this one Inſtance of it : That, although in preferring men to all other places
of the houſehold, I ever uſed to ask per-
miſſion firſt, (and accordingly was often
re-

refufed for the fake of *Roman Catholicks*, and others who were recommended by perfons more in favour than my felf) yet I was fo careful of keeping that confiderable part of the family unmix'd with mean or unworthy Chaplains (whom others I fear'd would have impos'd on his Majefty, againft his intention) that I conftantly fill'd up thofe vacancies, without giving him the leaft notice or trouble about it ; and fupply'd them with the ableft approved Divines I could poffibly find, moft commonly recommended to me by thofe Bifhops who were not of the Court. This I conceived the moft proper courfe in a matter concerning Clergymen, with a King of a different perfuafion from theirs ; and I intended it for his real fervice ; believing it had been better for that unhappy Prince, as well as the Kingdom, if the greater Ecclefiaftical Dignities had been difpos'd of by others with as much caution.

AND thus, *Sir*, I have endeavour'd to confirm you in your favourable opinion of me ; which muft be acknowledg'd by every body an approbation of fuch weight, that as I hope it may be an example of great

3

autho-

authority to many, so 'tis sufficient of it self to balance the censoriousness of others. *I am,*

S I R,

Your obliged humble Servant,

M U L G R A V E.

THE

Earl of *Mulgrave's*

SPEECH

In the HOUSE of LORDS,

FOR THE

Bill touching Free and Impartial Proceedings in Parliament.

THIS debate is of so great consequence, that I resolved to be silent, and rather to be advised by the ability of others, than to shew my own want of it; besides, it is of so nice a nature, that I who speak always unpremeditately, apprehend extremely the saying any thing which may be thought the least reflecting: though even that ought not to restrain a man here from doing his duty to the publick, in a business where it seems to be so highly concern'd.

I

I have always heard, I have always read, that foreign nations, and all this part of the world, have admir'd and envy'd the conſtitution of this Government. For not to ſpeak of the King's power, here is a Houſe of Lords to adviſe him on all important occaſions, about peace or war; about all things that may concern the nation, the care of which is very much entruſted to your Lordſhips. But yet becauſe your Lordſhips cannot be ſo converſant with the generality of the people, nor ſo conſtantly in the country as is neceſſary for that purpoſe, here is a Houſe of Commons alſo choſen by the very people themſelves, newly come from among them, or ſhould be ſo, to repreſent boldly all their grievances,. to expreſs the true mind of the nation, and to diſpoſe of their money, at leaſt ſo far as to begin all bills of that nature; and if I am not miſtaken, the very writ for elections ſent down to the Sheriffs, does impower them to chuſe. What? Their Repreſentatives. Now, my Lords, I beſeech you to conſider the meaning of the word *Repreſentative:* Is it to do any thing contrary to their mind? It would be abſurd to propoſe it; and yet how can it be otherwiſe, if they, after their being choſen, change their dependency, en

gage

gage themfelves in employments plainly inconfiftent with that great truft repofed in them. And that I will take the liberty to demonftrate to your Lordfhips they now do, at leaft according to my humble opinion.

I will inftance firft in the leaft and loweft incapacity they muft be under, who fo take employments.

YOUR Lordfhips know but too well what a general careleffnefs there appears every day more and more in the publick bufinefs: If fo, how is it likely that men fhould be as diligent in their duty in Parliament as that bufinefs requires, where employments, and a great deal of other bufinefs, fhall take up both their minds and their time?

BUT then in fome cafes 'tis worfe; as in Commands of the army, and other employments of that kind, when they muft have a divided duty: For it does admirably become an officer to fit voting away money in the Houfe of Commons, while his foldiers are perhaps taking it away at their quarters, for want of his prefence to reftrain them, and of better difcipline among them; nay, perhaps his troop or regiment may be in fome action abroad, and he muft either have the fhame of being abfent from them at fuch a time, or from that Houfe, where he is entrufted with all our Liberties. To this I have heard but one objection by a noble Lord, That if this act fhould pafs, the King is not allow'd to make a captain or a colonel, without difabling him to fit in Parliament, by fuch a commiffion.

TRULY, if a captain has only deferv'd to be advanced for expofing himfelf in Parliament, I think the nation would have no great lofs in the King's letting alone fuch a preferment.

BUT, my Lords, there is another fort of incapacity yet worfe than this; I mean that of Parliament-men's having fuch places in the *Exchequer,* as the very profit of them depends on the money given to the King in Parliament. Would any of your Lordfhips fend and entruft a man to make a bargain for you, whofe very intereft fhall be to make you give as much as he can poffibly?

IT puts me in mind of a *Farce,* where an actor holds a dialogue with himfelf, fpeaking firft in one tone, and then anfwering himfelf in another.

REALLY, my Lords, this is no *Farce*; for it's no laughing-matter to undo a nation:
But

But 'tis altogether as unnatural for a member of Parliament to ask firſt in the King's name for ſuch a ſort of a ſupply, give an account from him how much is needful towards the paying ſuch an army, or ſuch a fleet, and then immediately give, by his ready vote, what he had before ask'd by his maſter's order. Beſides, my Lords, there is ſuch a neceſſity now for long Seſſions of Parliament, and the very privileges belonging to members are of ſo great extent; that it would be a little hard and unequal to other gentlemen, that they ſhould have all the Places too, as well was the Privileges.

A L L the objections that have been made, may be reduced to theſe :

F I R S T 'tis told us, That 'tis a diſreſpect to the King, if his ſervants or officers be excluded.

T o this, I deſire it may be conſider'd, That 'tis in this caſe, as when a tenant ſends up any body to treat for him ; would any of your Lordſhips think it a diſreſpect, nay would the King himſelf think it any, if the tenant would not wholly refer himſelf to one of your own ſervants, or the King's commiſſioners in the caſe of the crown? And if he chuſes rather ſome plain honeſt friend of his own, to ſupply his abſence here ; will any

H 2 blame

blame such a proceeding, or think it unmannerly?

BESIDES, your Lordships know even this
Act admits them to be chosen, notwithstanding their employments ; provided the
Electors know it first, and are not deceived
in their choice.

ALL we would prevent, is, that a good
rich corporation should not chuse to entrust
with all their liberties, a plain honest country neighbour, and find him within six
months changed into a preferred, cunning
courtier ; who shall tie them to their choice,
though he is no more the same man than
if he were turn'd *Papist* ; which by the law,
as it stands already, puts an incapacity upon
him.

ANOTHER objection is, That this act
may, by its consequence, prolong this Parliament ; which they allow would be a very
great grievance ; and yet suppose the King
capable of putting it upon us: I have too
much respect for him to admit of this ; but
I am glad however that 'tis objected by
Privy-counsellors in favour ; who consequently, I hope, will never advise a thing,
which they now exclaim against as so great
a grievance.

BUT

But pray my Lords, what should tempt the King to so ill a policy ? Can he fear a freedom of choice in the people ; to whose good-will he owes all that power, which these Lords suppose he may use to their prejudice ?

THEREFORE give me leave to say, as I must not suspect him of so ill a design as the perpetuating this Parliament, so he cannot, he ought not to suspect a nation, so entirely (I was going to say so fondly) devoted to him.

My Lords, no man is readier than my self to allow that we owe the Crown all submission, as to the time of calling Parliaments according to law, and appointing also where they shall sit. But with reverence be it spoken, the King owes the nation entire freedom, in chusing their representatives ; and it is no less his duty, than his true interest, that such a fair and just proceeding should be used towards us.

CONSIDER, my Lords, of what mighty consequence it may be, that so many votes should be free, when upon one single one may depend the whole security or loss of this nation. By one single vote a general

ex-

excife may be granted, and then we are all loft. By one fingle vote the Crown may be impower'd to name all the Commiffioners for raifing the taxes, and then furely we fhould be in a fair way towards it.

NAY, whatever has happen'd may again be apprehended ; and I hope thofe reverend Prelates will reflect, that if they grow once obnoxious to a prevalent Party, one fingle voice may be as dangerous to that bench, as a general diffatisfaction among the People prov'd to be once in a late experiment : which I am far from faying by way of threat-ning, but by way of caution.

MY Lords, we may think, becaufe this concerns not the Houfe of Lords, that we need not be fo over-careful of the matter ; but there are Noblemen in *France*, at leaft fuch as were fo before they were enflav'd, who, that they might domineer over others, and ferve a prefent turn perhaps, let all things alone fo long, 'till the people were quite mafter'd, and the nobility themfelves too, to bear them company. So that I never met a *Frenchman*, even of the greateft rank (and fome had ten thoufand Piftoles a year in employments) that did not envy us here for

our

our freedom from that flavery which they groan under: And this I have obferv'd univerfally, except in Monfieur DE LOUVOIS, Monfieur COLBERT, or fuch people; becaufe they were the Minifters themfelves who occafion'd thefe complaints, and thrived by the oppreffion of others.

MY LORDS,

THIS country of ours is very apt to be provok'd; we have had a late experience: and though no wife man but would bear a great deal rather than make a buftle; yet really the people are otherwife, and at any time change a prefent uneafinefs for any other condition, tho' a worfe. We have known it fo too often, and fometimes repented it too late.

LET them not have this new provocation, in being debarred from a fecurity in their *Reprefentatives*. For malicious people will not fail to infufe into their minds, that all thofe vaft fums which have been, and ftill muft be raifed towards this war, are not difpofed away in fo fair a manner as ought to be; and I am afraid they will fay their money is not *given*, but *taken*.

I am fure, whatever fuccefs this Bill may have, there muft needs come fome good effect of it ; for if it paffes, it will give us *Security* ; if it be obftructed, it will give us *Warning*.

A

A
SPEECH
IN THE
HOUSE of PEERS,
April 18, 1695.

YOUR Lordfhips have fhewn me fo much juftice, and indeed fo much favour and patience, in your examination of this whole bufinefs at my humble requeft ; that I fhould make an ill return, if I wafted your time unneceffarily. And therefore I will not trouble you with obfervations on thofe unufual methods, odd aggravations, and inexcufable delays, that fome few perfons have openly practifed in this debate. I will not, I need not infift upon it ; your Lordfhips have all taken notice of it fufficiently ; and the truth is, fuch an over-eagernefs in a very fmall number againft the opinion of the reft, inftead of hurting me, only expofes themfelves. Yet I am forry for this odd manner of procceding, notwith-

withstanding all the advantage it has given
me : because it has also given occasion for
a malicious suspicion in this censorious town,
as if I had done these Lords some sort of
private injury ; of which yet I am so innocent, that they will not add it to their other
accusations against me, I am confident.

NEITHER will I take up your Lordships time with recriminations ; I confess it
is hard to hold, when 'tis so easy to do it ;
the subject is ample enough, and your Lordships will not think it so unbecoming a gentleman to return an accusation, as it was to
be the first accuser : but, tho' never so much
tempted, I have too much respect for this
great assembly to entertain you so ill.

THE only thing I shall trouble you with,
is the defence of what a man cannot be too
careful of, my honour ; and accordingly shall
tell your Lordships a true story very plainly.
If I should fail in any thing, it wou'd be no
wonder, since I have neither used counsel
without doors, nor troubled you with any
here ; being of opinion any man is able to
speak truth without any assistance.

ABOUT four years ago I design'd to build
a house, and therefore dispos'd of that I lived
in to the *Spanish* Ambassador ; inquir'd every
where

where for ground; treated with Mr. NEAL for his beyond *Berkley*-houfe, and with many others alfo; but at laft fixed on that fpot of ground you have now heard fo much of. Upon my propofing it to thofe concern'd, I found two difficulties; firft, the title was fo perplex'd, there was no buying without an Act of Parliament to clear it; the fecond was, that the inheritance of this ground after feventy four years is in the City of *London*. I endeavour'd to overcome the firft of thefe difficulties, by procuring an agreement among the proprietors in the prefent leafe of feventy four years, in order to have an Act of Parliament; and for the other, I treated with the City, defiring only four acres in all, for a houfe, a court before it, and a fmall Garden behind it. I think the firft time I propos'd it was here in the bifhops lobby to Sir———HUBLAND, Sir R. CLAYTON, and three more of the city all together, who then affur'd me the inheritance could not be parted with. Upon this I defir'd a leafe of one hundred and fifty years, which yet was refufed; and after many months I obtained one of one hundred years only.

WHILE this was treating above a twelvemonth, one of the city officers brought me

arti-

articles to sign; of which one was, that the lease should be void, unless I procur'd such an Act of Parliament to pass for settling all matters about it; wherein some clauses of his penning might be inserted for the City's advantage. This condition appear'd so unreasonable to me, (who was only one of the many parties that were to consent to such a private Act, before ever the Parliament, I knew, would pass it) that in a little heat I told this small officer Mr. LANE (the worthy witness) that it must be his own proposal, and too extravagant a one to come from the City, who had never asked such a condition. Mr. LANE grew excessive angry, as the other person then present has sworn; and very pertly told me he was not to be ruffled out of his care for the City by any subject whatsoever; and yet, to pacify the good man, who might by his place do ill offices by a misrepresentation, I agreed (not that an Act should pass, tho' a private one) but only that I would, as a party, give my consent to it as soon as all the other proprietors did so too. But the true reason why I refused his proposal, was not for the least doubt I had of your Lordships passing the Bill (which now lies on the table ready

drawn

drawn by Mr. FOULK's, who sent it at my request) but only because in justice your Lordships require all parties agreement to any private Bill, which I fear'd so many of them would hardly be persuaded to; and then my Grant from the City was to have been void, if I had sign'd his fine proposal.

To make an end of a long story, the City granted the Lease at last, and it lies also on your table, full of covenants so much to the City's advantage, and so little to mine, (there being some articles of charge to me besides the rent) that I have sold to the Lord JEFFREYES for one hundred guineas this great present of the City (of which some have made such a noise) because it is of no use to me without building my house; which design fails only for want of the mortgagee's being able to make a sure title; and they are not enough agreed to get an Act to pass about it. Upon this I will make a few remarks, and so conclude. First,

THE value of this is, you see, so very inconsiderable, that it alone answers all suspicion about it: For tho' a bribe of a meer bawble is inexcusable; yet when circumstances are examined in order to judge if it be a bribe, or not, I suppose a plain gold ring

3.

is

is not to be fufpected as much as a diamond of one thoufand pounds.

THE next objection vanifhes about my undertaking for this Act, when it is confidered how many inftances there are every day of members in both houfes who article, not only as I have done, to endeavour at, but alfo to procure a private Act of Parliament; becaufe indeed they can be underftood to mean no more by it, than to confent themfelves, to perfuade others what they can, and fometimes to pay the fees of the clerks, which in this very Leafe I am oblig'd to free the city from, whenever the Act paffes.

THE length of the Leafe is as odd a cavil as the reft; fince one hundred years is certainly as proportionable a term for fuch a great houfe, as forty years for a little one, efpecially confidering how flightly they build thofe little ones now-a-days.

WHEREAS there was fome mention of my obliging the city about GULSTON's Bill; I confefs my memory did not lay that value upon it, as it feems their gratitude did, who own'd the obligation. It appears to have been a private bill which invaded the City of *London*'s rights, againft which I deli-

deliver'd their petition, and made the matter fo plain, that your Lordfhips threw out the Bill.

It happen'd very lately, that an honeft country gentleman heard only by accident, of an Act's being like to pafs, which had undone him. I fancy if any Lord had ftopp'd it, either out of good will to him, or juftice; the gentleman would call that Lord his friend ever after, and drink his health too, in fpite of all his enemies.

Consider alfo the open manner of this whole proceeding with a great City, for at leaft a year together without interruption.

Each claufe ftood upon with all ftrictnefs, and every article difputed by counfel before them.

Before a committee of twelve common-council men, and fix aldermen deputed to manage fuch things.

Carried at laft there (I defire your Lordfhips will take notice of that remark, becaufe of a great eftate loft here lately by equal votes) not by an Equality; if fo, I fhould not wonder at a review taken of it; for things carried in that kind, will be talk'd of, and perhaps once more confidered. But

3   this

this was done, my Lords, by a great majority; it was fworn here at your Bar that there were but three againft it, and they too own'd to your Lordfhips themfelves, it was only becaufe they thought the ground worth ten pounds a year more; which being after feventy years to come, is to be valued at a year's purchafe; fo I have a notable bargain of ten pounds, according even to their oaths, who croffed me in it, becaufe indeed influenced by that City-officer.

OBSERVE alfo, if you pleafe my Lords, the City fent their officers feveral times to view this ground, by which one of my oppofers own'd here he was at laft convinc'd, that it was a good bargain for the City, upon account of their pipes and building.

AND now, my Lords, I have referv'd to the laft, what alone would vindicate this bufinefs. This very ground is in truftees names for the City, one of whom is an infant; fo, they could make me no legal title before he comes to age, and I have only an equitable one to depend on. Therefore when this is to be confirmed and made valid, the city muft be under other governors, who will never fure confirm an ill thing done by thefe: and they cannot be compelled to it, but in

the

the court of *Chancery*; which muft then review all this whole proceeding.

As to the Convex-Lights, your Lordfhips have feen I am not the leaft concern'd; but it falls out unluckily for my accufers, that they pretend I am too much regarded by fo great a City for affifting them on all occafions (which I fhall ever be proud of) and yet all the while blame me for ftopping their Orphans Bill by my only intereft here: A direct contradiction.

I have troubled your Lordfhips too long about fo flight a matter; which indeed was unneceffary; for though it happen'd once that many mifdemeanors amounted to a treafon, I am confident a thoufand flanders out of the mouth of what great man foever, will never here be able to give a fufpicion of mifdemeanor, unlefs of himfelf who flanders.

MY LORDS,

I am too often entertaining your Lordfhips on all other occafions; and perhaps fhould be too apt to do it in my own cafe, efpecially if any Lord fhould either object, or recite amifs; which in this debate has been found not impoffible. I ask your leave therefore to withdraw; not doubting but in such a case, my innocence will be safe under your Lordships protection, and much better defended than if I were here my self to look after it.

—————————

OBSER,

OBSERVATIONS

ON THE

Statute of Treasons,

Paſſed the 25th of EDWARD III.

OBSERVATIONS

ON THE

Statute of Treasons.

I AM fenfible it becomes me to be very circumfpect, when I advance any thing that is fingular in a part of learning, in which I have been fo little converfant: I fhall only therefore propofe my opinions, with the grounds for them, leaving their probability to be decided by others, whofe profeffion has qualified them to be proper judges.

1. THE firft article of this ftatute is about compaffing or imagining the King's death ; and upon that, my Lord COKE afferts a little oddly, in my humble opinion, that a perfon not *compos mentis*, and an *infant*, are neither of them to be comprehended within this ftatute, becaufe they cannot be fuppofed capable of any defign: And he fays farther,

I 3 That

That although by the ſtatute of 33 Hen. 8. a man falling mad after the fact, was to be try'd and attainted notwithſtanding ; and, if after the condemnation, was yet to be executed ; it was too cruel and inhumane a law to be long unrepeal'd.

I cannot but think this opinion of his a little extraordinary, becauſe of the great facility there may be either of an infant's being put upon committing a miſchief of this kind ; or of any perſon's counterfeiting madneſs for that very purpoſe : We know too, of how unlimited an age an infant in law is, provided he be under twenty one years. So that methinks, where ſo general and publick a miſchief is to be prevented, no loop-hole for eſcaping ought to be admitted.

A man's falling mad after ſuch a fact, is ſo ill an excuſe from puniſhment, that (beſides the great temptation of counterfeiting it) ſuch a diſorder of the brain may be very well ſuppoſed an uſual conſequence of ſo black a crime ; eſpecially when the criminal hears that dreadful ſentence which our law pronounces againſt it.

And if my Lord Coke's opinion in this caſe ſhould prevail, I believe few would ever die for treaſon ; ſince a man muſt be

really

really mad, not to affect it in such a case of neceffity. Neither do I fee why there fhould be fo great a tendernefs as is fuffi-cient to ballance the punifhing fo black a mifchief; for to one truly diftracted, death is not fo great an evil, as his fuffering may be a good to others by way of terrour and example.

2. 'T is no wonder the meer defign againft a King's life is treafon by this ftatute; fince, at the time of making it, the defign only of murdering any body was felony, and pu-nifh'd with death. This was the only diffe-rence; That, in cafe of a fubject, the ill defign was to appear by fome act of vio-lence, as wounding, &c. but in this cafe, any act whatfoever that proves fuch a de-fign, is fufficient. My Lord COKE is of o-pinion, That no *Words* are enough for being accounted an overt-act, unlefs fet down in writing by the criminal; in which I think he leaves it yet too general; becaufe wri-ting is almoft as fubject to mifconftruction, as fpeaking : though I confefs his inftance is a good one, of Cardinal POOL's exhor-tation to the Emperor for his invading *Eng-land* in HENRY the Eighth's time : which muft be allow'd to be a paramount overt-

act

act of treason, though he should have written but one letter about it.

3. I am a little unsatisfy'd also with another explanation of this act by my Lord COKE,
where he says that designing to depose, im-
prison, or take into one's power the King,
is within this statute ; and yet will not allow
a design of levying war to be so. For the
only reason which he gives himself, why
those first designs are within the statute, is
the great danger a King must needs be in,
when so deposed or imprisoned ; for the bare
words of the statute do not reach it : Now,
sure, the same inference, if a good one,
holds as well in this latter case ; since a
war levy'd against a King, may as well endanger his person, as either a deposition, or
an imprisonment. But the truth is, a meer
design of deposition, imprisonment, or levying war, are not within the bare words of
this law ; but yet the Judges in all times have
so over-rul'd it otherwise, that whosoever is
mischievous enough to be found guilty of
such ill designs, will, to his cost, find the
Judges as mischievous in stretching the law
against him ; though all the while they pretend to be of his Council.

4. ALL

4. ALL Lawyers are of opinion, that by this ftatute is meant even a King *de Facto*; for they fay a King *de Jure* may afterwards p unifh, according to this ftatute, any man who has for any caufe but his Title, confpired againft a King *de Facto*. The reafon of which feems to be good; fince the publick is more concern'd in having their peace and plenty difturb'd, than in preferring one King before another, or in determining the rights of the two *Rofes*. For I would fain know, if it had not been better for the poor people of *England* that fome third Branch had obtain'd the Crown from them both, and poffefs'd it quietly, than to be torn in pieces with fuch a Civil War as we cannot read without horror.

5. THE next Treafon in this Act is about violating the Queen; and the words are (*la Compagne du Roy*) which might be underdood of any Miftrefs a King fhould own publickly, if the weight of the crime lay only in difrefpect or injury to the King; but 'tis chiefly in the difturbance it may give the publick: and therefore the King's Wife only can be here underftood, becaufe the people are highly concern'd in his Iffue by her; but have nothing to do with his illegitimate

Children,

Children, or with thofe Women by whom he has them.

So alfo the Statute mentions only the King's eldeſt Daughter, and his eldeſt Son's Wife ; whereas the difrefpect to him would be as great in violating his fecond Daughter, or his fecond Son's Wife : But in that cafe the publick is not fo concern'd, on whofe account chiefly this Law was made, and not fo much out of regard to his Perfon or Dignity.

6. 'T I s generally taken for granted, and, as I remember, my Lord COKE himfelf fays, *That a Queen-Confort herfelf is within this Statute, if confenting to be enjoyed :* But I fee no ground for that opinion, except HENRY the Eighth's practice ; there being not a word of it in this Act.

A N D becaufe the Act provides no punifh-ment for a Queen, nor for either of thofe Princeſſes fo offending, I believe it is wholly miftaken, and by the word (violate) a Rape only is intended ; and confequently the wo-men cannot be guilty. For if it was meant otherwife, by what juftice or reafon fhould that fact (of love perhaps) draw fo great a punifhment on the man, while the woman whofe falfehood to the King augments her crime, and makes it a double treafon, yet by this Act wholly efcapes unpunifh'd ?

I

BESIDES;

BESIDES; what fault has the injur'd King done in such a case, that his cuckoldom is to be made publick, and every body is to endeavour the discovery of it under pain of misprision; and yet himself not freed from such an adulterous wife by any clause in this Law, which never mentions her as a criminal? By all which it appears, that a rape only is meant in this statute, (an injury indeed, but not so great a shame to the husband, according to the foolish custom of the world) as indeed the word (*violer*) implies; and had never been, I believe, interpreted otherwise, but for HENRY the Eighth, who, to get rid of two wives in his arbitrary way, stretch'd it to adultery: with which too he was not contented; but got a Law to pass, which made it Treason both in any woman he should ever marry, and in her Lover also, if they could be prov'd to have lain together formerly, and had not acquainted him with it before his marriage: which my Lord HERBERT says, did so frighten all the women, that he was forc'd to be contented with a widow at last; because others were afraid he might pretend to miss a maidenhead, and so cut off a wife's head, as soon as he grew weary of her.

UPON

UPON this occasion, I remember a pleasant difficulty which happen'd in the time of Queen ELIZABETH. An Act was drawn about establishing her issue; and the usual words of such statutes in her licentious Father's reign are (*issue lawfully begotten*). This appear'd to the Parliament a little unmannerly; so that the words (*issue lawfully begotten*) were chang'd into these (*natural born issue*) and sometime (*issue of her body*): but this being a variation of the customary phrase, it gave a jealousy among the people, that her great favourite LEICESTER intended to set up for King some bastard of his after her death, and pretend he was born of her, and bred up privately.

7. ANOTHER observation is, that by the word (*Compagne*) a Queen Dowager is excluded, according to the opinion of all Lawyers: yet this is not so clear, if we consider her to have been once (*la Compagne du Roy*) by which that word may reach her, especially within some time after her husband's death; for, during a possibility of being left *enceinte*, the reason of the Law will include her also as well as a King's wife, upon the publick account. All which is still a confirmation of the statute's meaning only a rape;

I

for

for elſe, not only a Queen, a King's eldeſt daughter, and his eldeſt ſon's wife, but the widows alſo, are moſt dangerous perſons to be approach'd, and even for ſome time after their husband's death ; which conſiſts not with the meaning of a Law that was intended altogether in favour of the ſubject, and for which *England* hath ſung encomiums of King EDWARD to this day.

8. THE next thing in it to be conſider'd, are theſe words (*the King's eldeſt Son and Heir*) by which copulative (*and*) he muſt be his Heir, as well as eldeſt ſon ; which ſuppoſes a poſſibility of altering by Act of Parliament the Line of Succeſſion, and taking it from the eldeſt.

9. 'TIS certainly meant alſo, that, unleſs the King's eldeſt daughter be unmarry'd, and conſequently more expos'd by wanting a husband's care, there is no Treaſon in the caſe ; for otherwiſe, a King's ſecond ſon's wife had been named before her, as being nearer the Crown : And this confirms it to be meant a rape all along, to which a ſingle woman is more liable than one probably marry'd to ſome foreign Prince. Whereas from the danger of an intrigue, I ſuppoſe thoſe wiſe Law-makers would hardly have
thought

thought her the more secure by marriage. If it be urg'd that both the other Ladies protected by this Law are wives, which lessens the force of my last argument; I desire it may be consider'd that all the care of those, is only upon account of their husbands, *viz.* the King, and Prince of WALES, in whom the publick is so much concern'd; but not at all for them, before they become those Princes wives: Whereas one so near the Crown as a King's eldest daughter, is in her own person of too great consequence, not to be guarded by this Law 'till she has a husband, who is then suppos'd capable of defending her himself against all such violent attempts.

IT may be objected, that if a rape only was meant, there was no need of this Law against it; because that crime committed against the meanest person was already punishable with death: but in this case the death is made more severe, and also the blood attainted.

10. As to the following Article, my Lord COKE has another odd opinion; That, altho' it comes within this statute, to assist the King's enemies; it does not reach those who assist rebels; because (he says) rebels cannot properly

perly be call'd enemies, but rather traitors. Accordingly he makes a great difference between the crimes of conspiring with a foreign Prince (which he accounts Treason) and of conspiring at home with other subjects to levy war (which he says is none, unless the war be actually made) which seems as if he allow'd a people, in some extraordinary cases, to project a remedy among themselves, but never to confide in, or join with, any stranger about it.

11. THE next Article is about counterfeiting the Great Seal, and Privy Seal; where both the Privy-Signet, and Sign Manual are left out, but added (I think unwisely) in a later statute.

12. CLIPPING, washing, and filing money for lucre sake, are also added since to the Treasons in this Act about money. But, tho' both these additions only supply what appears to be rather forgotten than left out of this statute; yet I wonder at those Parliaments that thought such inconsiderable things worth their breaking a gap for an addition of Treasons, after their wise ancestors had by this Law made such a fence against them, by taking away all those at the common Law:

13. BUT

13. But the most confiderable part of all this ftatute is the word (*provably*) a moft fignificant one; and yet in our printed Statute-books 'tis changed into the word (*probably*) one moft dangerous, and unintelligible, and worthy of a publick amendment in Parliament : For tho' 'tis rectify'd in the margin of KEBLE's collection ; fuch a wrong word foifted in, is a little fufpicious, and would hardly be continu'd fo long there by chance. Perhaps it has been thought there is more need of difcouraging all fuch attempts, than of fetting bounds to the Judges, or Jury ; but 'tis plain that King EDWARD the third was not of that mind.

14. The next thing is the claufe which makes it Treafon to kill the Chancellor, Treafurer, or any Juftice in doing his office; by which their perfons are not otherwife protected than in the execution of their employments : And the reafon why a King's perfon is made by this Law fo very facred at all times, is becaufe he is always executing his great office either by himfelf or his deputies; all acts of juftice running ftill in his name, who is ever fuppos'd to intend that right fhould be done even againft himfelf or favourites ; and therefore any failure of

it

it in thofe deputies is punifhable, notwithftanding any direction they may have from
him to excufe it.

. 15. T H E R E are three other Treafons
mentioned after this; of a wife's killing her
husband; a fervant his mafter; or a clergy-
man his prelate; on which I will only obferve, that a worfe than all thefe is omit-
ted; in imitation I fuppofe of old *Rome*,
which made no Law againft Parricides, becaufe they thought human villainy incapable
of arriving at fo great a height. But our
anceftors might have confider'd, that two
thoufand years are a great while for mifchief
to grow in, efpecially in thefe hot Climates
of Zeal and Enthufiafm.

16. N o w comes the moft important claufe
in this Act to be confider'd, which is in thefe
words. " And becaufe that many other
" like cafes of Treafon may happen in time to
" come, which a man cannot think nor de-
" clare at this prefent time, it is accorded,
" That if any other cafe, fuppofed Treafon,
" which is not above fpecify'd, doth happen
" before any Juftices; the Juftices fhall tarry
" without any going to judgment of the
" Treafon, 'till the caufe be fhew'd and de-

Vol. II.   K   " clar'd

" clar'd before the King and his Parliament,
" whether it ought to be judg'd Treaſon or
" Felony."

THERE has been ſo great a difference in
opinion about the true interpretation of this
clauſe, that I hope it is a little excuſable, if
(in a matter allow'd by all to be obſcure
enough) a man ſo ignorant of the Laws as
I am, ſhould happen to be as much in the
wrong as many others.

BUT, to begin with the ſeveral interpretations of this clauſe: Some will have it underſtood, that it gives a right to the judicial
power of the Houſe of Lords, to judge any
other facts Treaſon which they ſhall think
of ſuch ill conſequence to the publick, as
to deſerve that name, and the puniſhment
belonging to it. For, they ſay by the word
(Parliament) in matters of judicatory, is always meant the Houſe of Lords only; becauſe the other Houſe has nothing to do with
things of that nature, unleſs to accuſe and
bring offenders before the Lords to be tried.
And as to the King's being mention'd in the
clauſe; they pretend that 'tis only according to the form in all courts of judicature,
where the King is always ſuppoſed to be
virtu-

virtually prefent; efpecially in that fupreme Court, at the upper end of which his throne is ever under a canopy, and where he comes himfelf on all folemn occafions.

OTHERS are of opinion, That at this time when fuch care was taken to limit treafons, and retrench fo many as were before at the common Law, it could not be the meaning of that cautious Parliament, in the fame act of fecurity to the fubjects, to fet up an arbitrary power, tho' in the higheft Court, of making new treafons as often as the Judges fhould bring it before them: And therefore they conclude, fince thefe words (the King and his Parliament) are in their plain fignification (an Act of Parliament), and fince the reafon alfo appears to be on that fide, becaufe an Act for limitation of treafons would hardly eftablifh an unlimited power to declare new ones; that it ought to be thus underftood, *viz*. That fince there may happen crimes of fo dangerous a nature, as to appear before the Judges of equal guilt with thofe which are mention'd in this Act; yet they are here ftrictly forbid to meddle with them. So this claufe is an additional caution for the fecurity of the fubject, in re-

ftraining

ſtraining thoſe who are but too apt to make inferences of ſeverity, in flattery to that Government from which they expect advancement. But, at the ſame time, *in terrorem*, all is refer'd to a Parliament (King, Lords, and Commons) who, for extraordinary crimes againſt the publick good, may provide as unuſual puniſhments, by that arbitrary power which is ſafely entruſted no where elſe.

THESE two opinions have been argued very much of late years ſince the Earl of STRAFFORD's buſineſs; and they who maintain them, have yet agreed in this; that by that clauſe of King EDWARD, whatever caſe ſhall be determin'd either in the Lord's houſe (according to one opinion) or by an Act of Parliament (according to the other) that determination ſhall be a new ſettlement of the Law for the future; and that crime muſt be judg'd treaſon in *Weſtminſter-hall* for ever after, by force of this ſtatute of EDWARD the Third: And therefore (ſay they) to avoid that inconvenience of encreaſing the number of treaſons, that Act againſt the Earl of STRAFFORD expreſſly forbids it to go farther, or be a precedent to inferior Courts; without which caution, it muſt have been now

a

a settled treason for any man to say and do those things that were prov'd against that Earl; some of which are of so ambiguous a nature, that so prudent a Parliament was very much divided in the interpretation of them; and therefore universally agreed, that such a dubious case should never be subject to the determination of common Judges and Jury.

I know very well, at that time, (as 'tis usual in Parliament debates) and often since, it has been urg'd as a reproach to that proceeding against my Lord STRAFFORD, that even in the Act which destroy'd him, yet care is taken against any such severity for the future.

BUT that is a perfect mistake in some, and a meer fallacy in others; for the care of that Parliament for the future, in the cases of others, is only as I have expres'd it above, for fear the ordinary Courts below should follow, and perhaps mistake the precedent, according to this clause of EDWARD the Third: and not in the least to confine a future Parliament (which is impossible) or to censure themselves as doing a thing then, which even they who did it thought it too severe ever to be done again: For either of

K 3

those

thofe intentions, of confining a future Parliament, or of cenfuring themfelves, is fuch a weaknefs, as not only the Three Eftates of a Nation, but no three men in it are poffibly to be imagin'd capable of. Whereas it was very wife and juft in them to confider that, altho' by the neceffity of the times and iniquity of thofe arbitrary defigns in which my Lord of STRAFFORD was fo very able an inftrument, it was thought juft and fit to deftroy one man, in order to fave the whole; yet fuch a cafe was much too nice for inferior Judges to determine, or imitate them in; and therefore they reftrain'd them by that particular claufe in the Bill againft my Lord of STRAFFORD, which has made fo much noife in the world; but without which, it is very probable the Judges would have made as much mifchief.

BESIDES thefe two opinions of that claufe in the Act of 25 EDWARD III, there is another interpretation of it; which fuppofes, that it neither meant there fhould be an Act of Parliament to declare a new treafon, nor that one Houfe of Parliament alone fhould be trufted with fuch an arbitrary power; but that by the word (Parliament) is to be under-

understood the Two Houses together, which constitute it; with whom the King too is suppos'd to be virtually present, who yet have not power in themselves alone to declare a new treason, without authority given them by this clause. Whereas it was wholly unnecessary, in case an Act of Parliament was meant; because a King, Lords, and Commons (who must all join to pass an Act) have need of no such clause either to empower or defend them.

Tho' all these three opinions have been countenanc'd by very able men, I hope it will be no arrogance to make objections to them all. However, I shall have two of them still on my side, while I am disputing against the third.

The first opinion was that of the House of Lords only being meant in this clause; with which I must needs differ, tho' unwillingly, for these reasons.

First, Because so great and arbitrary a power as this, can never be suppos'd given by Three Estates to only one of them; by which the lives and fortunes of all the subjects in *England* would be at the disposal of the Peers.

SE,

SECONDLY, Becaufe in thofe leffer cafes of appeals from *Chancery*, and Writs of Error, where only money is concern'd; yet it may be obferv'd, that even there an arbitrary decifion of the Lords is fubmitted to, only that it may be taken from the Chancellor and the Judges: And indeed by fetting up an affembly to which we may in thofe cafes appeal, the fubjects are not expos'd, but rather fecur'd againft too much power in the *Chancery*, and in other Courts below.

THIRDLY, Tho' it muft be confefs'd, that by the word (Parliament) is fometimes meant only the Houfe of Lords; as when caufes are faid to be brought into Parliament, or the like; yet that is only becaufe the other Houfe has nothing to do in fuch matters, and therefore it needs no explanation: and 'tis the fame when we fpeak of Elections to Parliament, where the Houfe of Commons alone muft needs be underftood, becaufe there are no Elections into the other Houfe. But how is it poffible that in a new Law, and of the greateft importance imaginable, and for the quiet fettlement of all people's minds for the future, it should be meant of one Houfe only, and yet exprefs'd

ambi-

ambiguoufly, or rather indeed plainly to the contrary, by the word (Parliament) which is an affembly neceffarily compos'd of two Houfes?

I can imagine no reply will be made to this, unlefs it could be pretended that in the time when this Act was made, the word (Parliament) always fignified the Houfe of Lords only; even juft as the word (Peers) does now: But it is manifeftly the contrary in all the hiftories and records of that age.

THE *Second* opinion was, That by thefe words (the Judges fhall tarry till the caufe be fhew'd and declar'd before the King and his Parliament) it is intended there fhould be a new Act of Parliament in any fuch cafe, before the party be condemn'd; and after that, the Judges and Juries fhall find the fame fact Treafon ever after.

Now to this I have thefe objections.

1*ft*, THERE is nothing in thefe words importing any obligation on the Judges after the cafe hath once been ftated, and brought into Parliament; they are only directed to ftay proceedings, and to bring it hither.

AND 2*dly*, If the Judges had been fo oblig'd, yet that had been a good argument
againft

againſt our interpreting it to be meant of an Act of Parliament, and ſo one part of this opinion deſtroys the other: For, to what purpoſe ſhould a Parliament in EDWARD the Third's time authoriſe, or direct all future Parliaments? 'Tis authoriſing, to declare that what thoſe Parliaments enact, ſhall be Law; and it is directing, to ſay, That whenever ſuch Law ſhall paſs, inferiour Courts ſhould act ever after by the ſame meaſure. Whereas certainly the prudence of a preſent Parliament is likely to judge better of what new power ſhould be then given the Judges, than one in EDWARD the Third's time, ſo many hundred years before any ſuch new crime was committed.

THE other interpretation of this clauſe was, That both Houſes were meant by the word (Parliament) for, ſay they, it was needleſs to authoriſe King, Lords, and Commons, who have always an unlimited power; and it had been giving too great an authority to one Houſe only, viz. the Houſe of Lords; and therefore the meaning muſt needs be, that a Parliament compos'd of both Houſes ſhould interpret all ſuch caſes which are too hard for the Judges, and not expreſs'd in this Law plainly enough for them to preſume to meddle with it.   N o w

Now this perhaps would be a plaufible interpretation, if the words had not been (before the King and his Parliament.) For, tho' to the firft opinion of its being meant of the Houfe of Lords only, the mentioning a King is no objection; becaufe his name is always ufed in a Court of Judicature, where he is fuppofed to be virtually prefent; and becaufe *Weftminfter-hall* it felf where the Judges fate was anciently a part of that houfe where the King liv'd : Yet to thofe who take it to be meant of both Houfes, it is a very good objection; becaufe there is no colour of reafon for the King's being fo nam'd in the claufe, if the two Houfes are enabled by it to declare new Treafons without him, and perhaps even againft his opinion.

THE two Houfes of Parliament have certainly a very great authority as well as credit in this nation; and whatever they concur in, will bear fuch a weight along with it, as to break through almoft any oppofition. But yet there are bounds fet even to the Royal Prerogative, and to the two Houfes alfo; by which no alteration is allow'd to be made by them alone in any Law, much lefs in this the moft important of all our Laws.

Laws. An Act too sacred to be changed by any power less than omnipotent; I mean the Legislature, consisting of King, Lords, and Commons joined together.

But now my greatest task begins; and I find it much easier to make objections, than to establish any thing that shall be liable to none. However, if I went no farther in a matter of so much difficulty, it may be of some use to expose all erroneous interpretations; since any positive mistake of this clause is fatal, and a thousand times more dangerous, than a modest doubtfulness under so great an uncertainty.

Yet because it may be of some little use to my self, and cannot in the least be prejudicial to others; I am resolv'd to guess a little what the meaning of this oraculous clause should be, which runs in these words: (" And because that many other like cases " of Treason may happen in time to come, " which a man cannot think nor declare " at this present time; it is accorded, That " if any other case, supposed Treason, which " is not above specify'd, doth happen before " any Justices, the Justices shall tarry without " going to judgment of the Treason, 'till " the cause be shew'd and declar'd before " the

" the King and his Parliament, whether it
" ought to be judg'd Treafon or other Fe-
" lony.")

FIRST then it is agreed by all Lawyers,
that one of the beft ways of finding out the
meaning of an obfcure Law, is examining
well the Preamble to it, which in this is very fhort, as well as the Act it felf, and runs
in thefe words, (" Whereas divers opinions
" have been before this time, in what cafe
" Treafon fhall be faid, and in what not ;
" the King, at the requeft of the Lords and
" of the Commons, hath made a declara-
" tion in the manner as hereafter follow-
" eth.") By which it appears plainly, that a
wife Parliament, and a good King as wife
alfo as themfelves, intended to put an end
to all uncertainty in matters of Treafon ;
than which nothing can be more dangerous
to a People's quiet, and confequently to a
King's. This uncertainty was partly for want
of a Statute-law ; the Common-law being
made up of Precedents only, fome good,
and fome ill ; and partly from the different
tempers, or occafions of Princes, with which
the Judges are always too apt to comply.

BUT it had been directly contrary to fo
good a defign, if they had made this claufe

I   in

in the fenfe that moft underftand it, which
is this; That if a poor man (juft cautious
enough to avoid all the Treafons in this Act,
and yet perhaps not fo prudent as he fhould
be) falls into fome unufual fault, he fhall
bear the heavieft of punifhments by virtue of
a Law which he could never underftand, becaufe the crime muft be declared after his
fact is committed.

SECONDLY, What appears in nature more
oppofite to a law of indulgence and fecurity
(as this certainly is, notwithftanding its being
penal) than to put all our lives and fortunes
into the arbitrary power either of the Lords,
or Lords and Commons together.

I allow that, if the King's confent be added to that of both Houfes, all thofe three
Eftates in conjunction ought to be arbitrary:
And no body has a right to complain of
the legiflative power, in which himfelf has
a fhare.

BUT, tho' that interpretation of the claufe
is the moft confiftent with this Preamble of
fafety to the fubjects, who can be in no danger of injuftice from the legiflative power,
tho' never fo arbitrary : Yet 'tis wholly inconfiftent with reafon, that a Parliament in
EDWARD the Third's reign fhould intend to
advife

advife all future Parliaments ; by declaring that fome like cafes may happen in their time, and deferve their paffing a new Law about it. For advice it can only be, fince it would have been equally unneceffary and abfurd, for one Parliament to have pretended to give authority to another.

WHAT then fhould be the meaning of this claufe, about which our little world has made fuch a buftle?

IN my humble opinion, no more than this.

A wife King and Parliament forefaw, that a limitation of Treafons was fo great an indulgence, as poffibly to be made ill ufe of by fome who did not deferve it ; and yet, to their eternal honour, they preferr'd a general eafe and quiet, even to that and all other confiderations. But to keep bufy people the more in awe, who would efcape by the favour of this Act from any condemnation of Treafon, they hung out a flaming fword over their heads in this claufe ; which in truth is only minatory, and nothing elfe. That fo the Judges being commanded to tarry, and not to give any fentence in enormous cafes (which after this Law, could not be fo fevere as perhaps fome cafes might

I   deferve)

deferve) ill perfons might be the more ap-
prehenfive of a Parliament's heavier and more
arbitrary punifhment, whenever they did any
unufual crime to provoke it. For that method would have been againft the rules of
juftice, in trying a criminal twice for the
fame offence, unlefs they had by this claufe
oblig'd the Judges to tarry, and fufpend the
caufe 'till the fitting of a Parliament.

By which laft words it may be obferv'd
alfo that frequency of Parliaments was a thing
of courfe in thofe times, as much almoft as
the four Terms are now for affairs of a more
private nature.

But fince I underftand this claufe to be
only Minatory, in order to deter and not
to punifh offenders; it will be objected that
if this opinion were right, there had been
no occafion for all that caution, which I
my felf had juft now obferv'd in the Bill
againft my Lord of STRAFFORD.

I muft therefore take notice of an error
fo very general, that I am almoft afraid to
encounter it with my fingle opinion.

'T is commonly believ'd that by this claufe
in the Act of the 25th of EDWARD III, the
Judges are empower'd to hold and declare
in their courts to be Treafon, whatfoever

ever crimes shall be at any time judg'd Treason in Parliament. As for example, JOHN KERBY a mercer and JOHN ALGORE a grocer of the city of *London*, in the time of RICHARD II, had kill'd JOHN IMPERIAL, a publick Minister from the State of *Genoa*; and the Parliament happening to be sitting, pass'd an Act 3 RICHARD II. that they should be attainted of High Treason in the *King's Bench*; and they were executed accordingly. It was said, that all Judges after this were oblig'd to hold for Treason the killing any foreign Minister in the same manner, notwithstanding it is none of those crimes recited in the Act of 25 EDWARD III. And the only reason they gave for this opinion is the clause aforementioned, which therefore I will repeat again; (" And because that many other
" like cases of Treason may happen in time to
" come, which a man cannot think nor de-
" clare at this present time; it is accorded,
" That if any other case, suppofed Treason,
" which is not above specified, doth happen
" before any Justices, the Justices shall tarry
" without any going to judgment of the Trea-
" son, 'till the cause be shew'd and declar'd be-
" fore the King and his Parliament whether it
" ought to be judg'd Treason or other Felony.')

Now I believe no man in the word unprejudiced with a former opinion, will understand these words otherwise than thus. That, however enormous the cases shall happen to be, the Judges shall never go beyond the bare letter of this Law, but leave all to the safer judgment of Parliament.

And if a Parliament upon an extraordinary occasion, as that of the *Genoa* Embassador, shall in their great prudence inflict any unusual punishment; by what colour of reason should that be construed, as if they would have all the ordinary Judges hereafter do the same thing, without tarrying for their judgment?

One Parliament's proceeding is the best sort of precedent for another : But that it should be an example for inferiour Courts, is as preposterous and dangerous, as if a Schoolmaster should imitate a General, and instead of whipping a scholar, should put him to death by a general council of school-boys.

Besides, the very meaning of the clause is only to restrain the forwardness of inferiour courts; and yet this absurd interpretation enlarges their authority; by which it is not hard to guess how it comes to be encourag'd.

Add to this also, that supposing it were fit to enlarge their power of judging any new
offence,

offence, why fhould not the fame Parliament which firft determines that offence, determine alfo what new power the Judges fhould have concerning it ? whereas by their interpretation it muft be underftood, as if a Parliament in EDWARD the Third's time undertook to judge of new cafes that might happen in ours, and increas'd the jurifdiction of future Judges in all thofe yet unknown cafes.

UPON this vulgar error, the Parliament in my Lord of STRAFFORD's cafe, (being compos'd of fome members infected with it, and of others who found it neceffary to fatisfy thofe members as well as the reft of the world in their fears about it) *ex abundanti cautela*, added this claufe in that Act againft the Earl of STRAFFORD; (" Provided that " no Judge or Judges, Juftice or Juftices " whatfoever, fhall adjudge or interpret any " Act or Thing to be Treafon, in any other " manner than he or they, fhould, or ought " to have done before the making of this Act, " and as if this Act had never been or made.")

THIS was fo prudent a caution in that time of prefumptuous Judges, (in imitation of the like wifdom exprefs'd in an Act of the firft of Queen MARY) that it ought not to be blam'd : tho' it has accidentally con-

L 2   firm'd

firm'd many in their miſtake about the Judges power, after that Act was paſs'd, if this Proviſo (laſt repeated) had not prevented it.

But certainly, if the Act of Edward the Third placed no ſuch power in the Judges; this clauſe againſt any ſuch power, brought in for the greater caution, is far from giving a new interpretation to that Law, or any ſuch addition; eſpecially ſo dangerous a one as this would be.

It is not altogether foreign to this matter, if I obſerve another very common miſtake about that Bill againſt my Lord of Strafford. Abundance of people, eſpecially the old *Cavaliers*, underſtand this Proviſo laſt recited as a reflection on the Bill it ſelf; and as if his caſe was ſo very hard even in the opinion of the Parliament it ſelf, that it was ordered by this clauſe to be no precedent for the future.

This is a ridiculous error in many reſpects: Firſt, Becauſe doing a thing in one Parliament, and ordering it to be no precedent to another, is an errant bull; ſince the very doing it, is, and muſt be a precedent at the ſame time 'tis ordered that it ſhall be none. Secondly, It would have been an unparallell'd open injuſtice, to put one man to death

death for fuch a crime, as even in the opinion of thofe who punifh'd him, was not great enough to be capital in any other perfon, or at any other time. And it will not weaken this argument to fay, That it was an unjuft, cruel Act, and therefore a good many diffented from it : For thofe diffenting members themfelves could not be fo uncharitable as to imagine all the members of both Houfes who pafs'd the Bill, not only fo bafe and bloody as to be all the while againft it in their confciences, but fo foolifh alfo as to own it in the very Bill it felf. And therefore nothing can be plainer than that 'tis only a grofs miftake among ignorant people, to think they meant it in that manner.

ACCORDINGLY, that Act of CHARLES II, which has revers'd this Bill of Attainder, and in the Preamble recited every thing imaginable in favour of that Earl, yet takes no notice of this claufe, which had more difcredited the Bill than all the reft, if it could have been interpreted in that manner.

THE laft claufe in the Bill is about Highway-men, who had formerly been condemn'd for Traitors, only to inveft the Crown with their forfeited eftates. Here it is moft juftly provided, that hereafter they fhall only fuf-

fer

fer as felons, or trespassers, according to the
known Laws in those cases; and all such ill-
gotten estates are again restored by the Crown.
Which is another remarkable instance of the
benign intention of those wise Legislators,
shining almost in every word of this famous
Law.

I would not have communicated these
rambling thoughts to any but a friend; nor
to your self neither; if, among the several
misinterpretations upon my resigning one great
Employment, and refusing a greater, you had
not suspected me of a little laziness; from
which I hope this way of imploying my
leisure, may be some vindication; and I
wish it does not prove a much greater, by
shewing I needed no other reason besides my
disability, for not accepting the highest Post
in a profession I was never bred to; an honour too much, to think any man fit for,
except a Lawyer.

TWO
DIALOGUES.

A DIALOGUE

BETWEEN

Auguſtus Cæſar,

AND

CARDINAL RICHELIEU.

Aug. WHAT's the meaning of all this ceremony? Can wiſe men turn fops after they are dead?

R. SURE, 'tis impoſſible to pay too much reſpect to the great *Auguſtus.*

Aug. I was ſo cloy'd with it in the other world, that I cannot endure it yet, tho' it be ſo long ago; and beſides, among equals, as we are all here, what can be more propoſterous?

R. INDEED, if it were to your rank, you would have reaſon to ſay ſo; but I was never guilty of much ſubmiſſion that way.

Aug.

Aug. No: Your own King *Lewis* XIII. will clear you of that fault.

R. I confefs I defpis'd him always for his flothfulnefs and incapacity ; and from the fame caufe proceeds all my reverence to you; for no man ever knew fo well how to fatiffy himfelf, and the world too, at the fame time.

Aug. I did make indeed a pretty good figure, and truly you have made no ill one: Come, let us fit down together under thefe fhades.

R. Not *to be alive again:* What! fit cheek by jole with the wife, the happy Augustus! the perfection of prudence, the pattern of Princes, and admiration of all the world for thefe feventeen hundred years!

Aug. Sure you think you are wheedling your own Lewis ftill. What titles are here to no manner of purpofe ? What have I done to deferve all thefe fulfome complements ?

R. What have you not done ? Is it nothing to get the government of the whole world into your hands before you were twenty years old, and make it happy under that government, till you died at fourfcore? But yet,

yet, to shew you I mean no compliments, I have one objection even to you.

Aug. I thought at last the haughty Cardinal RICHELIEU would have some exception to any body that was above him.

R. AND you to any body that would not let you be so.

Aug. I find we know one another as well as if we had liv'd in the same age.

R. BUT we agree a little better: After all, I really admire you of all the Princes that ever reign'd. But yet——

Aug. BUT what?

R. SHALL I speak freely?

Aug. ON condition I may do the same.

R. AGREED. Then with your leave I must tell you, the world has had just cause to accuse you of two the greatest crimes imaginable, ingratitude and cruelty; and tho' I was myself inclined to the last, yet when joined with the first, I, and all mankind abhor it.

Aug. TWO heavy faults indeed; and if guilty, all the greatness I had, was not worth the buying it at so dear a rate.

R. PERHAPS you think so now indeed.

Aug.

Aug. WELL, 'tis eafy to guefs what you mean; but you little imagine how well I can clear myfelf.

R. INDEED I cannot; fince, with reverence be it fpoken, for all your mighty fame, your word will not pafs one jot in this matter.

Aug. YES it fhall, as I will order it.

R. HOW fo? Is it enough for a criminal to deny his crime?

Aug. YES, if he confeffes enough befides to condemn him: I will difcover a thoufand follies (which among us politicians are the faults we are moft afham'd of) rather than lie under this afperfion any longer. But I will make one condition.

R. WHAT?

Aug. THAT you will confefs as ingenuoufly how you came by all your greatnefs; for among friends, you and I know 'tis not to be gotten honeftly.

R. WELL, well, if it may go no farther.

Aug. NOT to the other world, you may be fure.

R. YOU have given me fo much curiofity and impatience to know your true Story, that in return, I will tell you mine more

fin-

sincerely than ever I did to my Confes-
sor.

Aug. OR else I should not be much the
wiser : For I suppose, that christian trick of
getting out secrets, did not pass on you. I'll
begin then. You must know, the world has
been mistaken in me throughout ; but 'tis no
wonder, for the very age I liv'd in, never
knew me.

R. I thought AUGUSTUS CÆSAR had been
no such obscure person.

Aug. OR else I had never been so famous. The *Romans,* as knowing as they
were, never understood me right ; they did
me much honour on one hand, and as much
wrong on the other. They all thought me
so wise, to mind nothing but my interest ;
and so wicked, as to sacrifice all things in
nature to it, even those who had most oblig'd me.

R. WHY, between friends, that is counted
no such great fault among us politicians.

Aug. IT may be then, you will count it
my folly, not to be ill-natur'd enough.

R. I am not very apt to suspect you of
that fault. But pray go on.

Aug. THE first part of my life is famous
for my being too hard for all the world be-

fore

fore I was fcarce a man; and infamous for yielding up CICERO to MARK ANTONY.

R. RIGHT: Thefe are the two things that eftablifh your character of being very wife, and very ungrateful.

Aug. I really was neither. CICERO did all for me in the gaining that power, which AGRIPPA and MECENAS managed fo well afterwards.

R. IN that you confefs all your obligations to CICERO; and truly you return'd them very well: what do you call ingratitude, if this be not fo?

Aug. NOTHING lefs, as you fhall hear prefently. I was a raw young heir to the greateft man that ever was; and all his army join'd with his party to buoy me up, almoft whether I would or no.

R. 'TWAS a fad thing, really to be fo ravifh'd.

Aug. FOR all your raillery, it might have proved fo, if CICERO had not wanted fomebody to fet up againft ANTONY.

R. To be capable only of being rival to fo great a man, was fufficient proof of your ability.

Aug. NOT at all, confidering the extravagant imprudence of my enemy, and the

I

pro-

profound policy of my friend; who having once fet up my reputation, AGRIPPA and MECENAS made it their whole bufinefs to improve it.

R. WERE they fo good Minifters?

Aug. THE ableft, I believe, that ever prince had, and almoft juft contrary in every thing to thofe you have known in later ages.

R. TRULY, that is commendation enough; but ftill 'tis a fign of your great prudence, to have chofen your Minifters fo well, and continued conftant to them fo wifely.

Aug. WILL you have the truth of it? I was all along in love with MECENAS's wife; and AGRIPPA marry'd my daughter.

R. BUT it was no fuch eafy matter, I believe, to make them agree always, in order to your greatnefs.

Aug. IT was for their own too; for they having different talents, one govern'd all the military affairs, and the other the civil; fo that being very wife men, they never clafh'd together like your petty States-men of late days, who think of nothing but ruining one another.

R. BUT ftill you fate at the helm, and govern'd all.

Aug.

Aug. Yes, but it was so calm most commonly, that I might have slept and done it; for all those good regulations in *Rome* and elsewhere, were only the projects of those admirable Counsellors.

R. 'Tis a more difficult thing than you make it, to have always an able Council.

Aug. Not if they happen well at first, and live a long time afterwards.

R. Yes, to maintain them in power against all their envious enemies.

Aug. It was they maintain'd me so. And now I have for truth's sake debased myself so much in your esteem; 'tis time I should a little recover it again, in regard to the Ingratitude you have accused me of; for 'tis only on that account I have confessed all this so freely.

R. You have own'd so much against yourself hitherto, that I am bound to believe now whatever you say.

Aug. Thus it was then; Cicero, with all his praises, never meant me well; and I once intercepted a letter of his, wherein he declared, I was the fittest person of all *Rome*, to be raised, to be advanced, and then at last to be destroyed.

R.

R. So what he only faid againſt you, you did againſt him ; 'tis a little hard to be taken at one's word ſo exactly.

Aug. You run on in a miſtake ; for not-withſtanding all this, he had made me ſo fond of him by his flatteries, that I abſolutely re-fus'd to ſign the proſcription while his name was there.

R. You would make me believe that he is yet alive, if I did not ſee him here every day ſhaking his head (which you cut off) at your going by him ſo confidently.

Aug. He judges, as all *Rome* did, that I connived at his death ; when all the while I had like to have loſt the world for his ſake, as Antony did afterwards for Cleopatra's.

R. You will tell me preſently you were as much in love with him, as he was with her.

Aug. Antony over-reach'd me in the matter, by giving me all the aſſurances ima-ginable that he would ſpare him for my ſake, if I would ſet him down in the roll for his : and ſo at once cunningly ſatisfied his revenge, and blacken'd me to all poſterity. But I think I was even with him.

R. Was this your quarrel ? I thought it was about you Siſter. Why did not you let the world know this ſtory, to juſtify your-ſelf?

Aug. I was really aſham'd of being us'd ſo like a child; and my friends told me it would never be believ'd, ſince LEPIDUS (who was the only perſon preſent) durſt not diſoblige MARK ANTONY with declaring the truth; for which I was reveng'd of him alſo.

R. THEN, inſtead of being ſo baſe as to ſacrifice your beſt friend to your ambition, it ſeems you fought afterwards more to revenge his death, than your Siſter's injuries.

Aug. JUST ſo: And ANTONY will own all this, for he laughs at me ſtill for it.

R. YOU may give ſuch a loſer leave to laugh a little. And does LEPIDUS laugh too? If they do, they are the merrieſt Ghoſts in *Elyſium,* for methinks they have no ſuch great cauſe.

Aug. No: LEPIDUS cries ſtill for the loſs of his Army, which left him for me, no-body knows why.

R. EXCEPT yourſelf; who I ſuppoſe had laid the buſineſs ſo before-hand.

Aug. WHY, there 'tis: Every thing which ſucceeds, is attributed to prudence. But be-lieve me, there is a great deal more of luck than

than skill, in our game of policy; and the worst players sometimes have the better success.

R. So it seems by you; I will never depend on History again.

Aug. 'Tis not so much the fault of History, as your false comments upon it.

R. True: For when once a prepossession is over, how one's eyes are open'd! I begin now to recollect a thousand things, which might have before convinc'd me of your being no such Solomon. Did you not marry a woman, while she was big with child by another man yet alive.

Aug. I confess it was an odd way of adopting a child into my family: But I lov'd her belly, big as it was, so well, that I could not endure any body else should have any thing more to do with it, tho' it were but to bring her to bed.

R. Then to bemoan yourself in the senate-house, for your Daughter's playing the whore.

Aug. Mecenas was dead, or else I had never done so foolish a thing. I remember as well as if it were but yesterday, how the very gravest Senators sneer'd at me to my very face.

R.

R. THEN, to be fo uxorioufly led by the nofe all your life.

Aug. NOT altogether fo neither; it was rather by another part; for LIVIA's temper and great prudence ingag'd me almoft always to be of the fame mind with her, which the malicious world mifcall'd being govern'd by her.

R. YOU were then ungrateful to her; for you grudg'd her the harmlefs pleafure of feeing young fellows run naked about the ftreets, 'till fhe wheedled you to believe they were no more regarded by her than fo many ftatues.

Aug. THAT was enough too; and, on my confcience, fhe fpoke equivocally: for now I think on't, fhe lov'd ftatues extremely well, and had a great collection.

R. OH, I remember now: MECENAS ufed you at a fine rate, when in a little note he call'd you *Murderer,* and bid you come down from the feat of judgment, where I fuppofe you were doing fome barbarous injuftice.

Aug. HAVE you heard that too? Why the truth of it is, a criminal there had put me into a paffion, a little unbefeeming a Judge; which as foon as ever that note had made me fenfible of, I left the trial immediately, for fear

of

of doing injuftice in my anger; which, by the way, is fome proof of my not being fo ill-natur'd, as I am thought to be.

R. No, nor fo very prudent neither, to be in paffion on thofe occafions. But, *Murderer*, that was a little familiar.

Aug. Well, but *Cuckold*, that excufes all things: befides, you may fee by that action what care he took of my reputation.

R. But above all the reft; your making Tiberius your fucceffor rather than one of your own family, is, I confefs, fomething fo extraordinary, that when I admir'd you moft, I could not excufe it.

Aug. Neither can I do it now. What would you have more? I confefs myfelf impos'd on all my life; moft commonly well, but at my death fo ill, that I am yet afham'd of it.

M 3 A

A DIALOGUE

BETWEEN

MAHOMET,

AND THE

Duke of Guise.

M. COME let us fit down here, and laugh a little together at all thofe tricks you and I have put upon the world.

G. WITH all my heart: What better ufe could we have made of it? Is mankind fit for any thing elfe but to be coufened?

M. YET you muft confefs that my way is the more noble, and had fomething of the fublime in it; you did your bufinefs by nothing but meer cringeing.

G.

G. YOU are miftaken : There goes more to popularity than that comes to ; and yet the cringeing you fpeak of, when 'tis of the Mind, is no fuch eafy matter.

M. NOT to fo lofty a one as yours, per_haps ; low ftooping makes a tall man's back ake.

G. YOU are merry, Sir, and therefore I fuppofe will not be loth to confefs fome of your noble tricks, as you call them.

M. ON condition you tell yours.

G. AGREED, and pray begin : Mine was but lay-diffembling, which ought to give place to divine-hypocrify.

M. YOU have heard of my Pigeon, I war_rant.

G. YES, and of your Owls too : Could fuch a grofs thing pafs among them ?

M. As eafily as a Creed : Nay, at laft, I might have fpared my pains of teaching the pretty bird ; for the rabble would have fancied her at my ear, tho' fhe had been all the while fluttering in their faces.

G. NAY, tho' fhe had been picking out their eyes. For I muft acknowledge you the beft of all the Bigot-makers that ever I read of ; my fuperftitious coxcombs never reach'd either the devotion, or morality of yours.

M.

M. THAT is, becaufe I laid a better bait than any in your Legends. Do you think there is any refifting the enjoyment of beautiful women with great eyes, for fifty years together? Is not that more defirable, than paffing through flames of purgatory, to only fpiritual imaginary pleafures?

G. BUT fure our joys unfpeakable are above even yours, which indeed in decency ought to have been unfpeakable too.

M. HAVE a care of that; 'twill never do. Whatever is unfpeakable, is alfo unconceivable. But this was not your fault, the fchoolmen fhould have mended it.

G. ABUNDANCE of them have try'd to do it.

M. BUT to no purpofe. 'Tis fuch a patch'd bufinefs, between the fuperftitions of old *Rome* and new *Rome* blended together, that the wife at laft were afham'd to wear it, and did as good as throw it quite off, by what they call'd a Reformation.

G. VERY well, Sir. But is any thing fo ridiculous as your lyes?

M. YES, your Legends. But fhall I confefs a truth will make amends for all my Lyes?

G. THAT will be fomething difficult.

M.

M. I began to believe them my self at laſt.

G. Oh ridiculous!

M. I was ſo very fortunate, that I fancied my ſelf a kind of favourite of Heaven; and if I had been put to it, 'tis not impoſſible but I might have died a martyr for a religion of my own invention.

G. THIS is more incredible than any thing in your whole *Alcoran.*

M. THEN, for all your popularity, you are not much skill'd in mankind. Why, we are all but over-grown children, afraid in the dark of our own ſcare-crows; and as fond too ſometimes of the babies we our ſelves trick up.

G. Is it poſſible?

M. YES, to flatter a man into any thing; ALEXANDER himſelf, that pupil of ARISTOTLE, and the very top of all humanity, did at laſt believe that JUPITER was really his father; and by his ſaying that ſleep and luſt convinc'd him of his being mortal, 'tis plain he ſometimes doubted it.

G. LIKE enough. And did your inſtruments SERGIUS the Monk, and the reſt, believe themſelves too?

M. RELI-

M. RELIGIOUS fort of men, you know, out-do all others in flattery; and I having fet them up for my ends, they fanctified me for theirs, 'till we almoft acted our felves into a real veneration for one another. But tell me now a little of your pranks, for you play'd them, I hear, to fome purpofe.

G. I had fo, if the bufinefs at *Blois* had not prevented me.

M. BUT you had a fine time of it 'till then.

G. VERY far from it. Rowing in the Gallies is nothing to the toil of popularity; but ambition is rebutted with nothing.

M. WHY, pray where was all this trouble?

G. FIRST, I never faid one word I thought, and pafs'd all my life in gaining fuch People's affections, whom all the while I contemn'd for being deceiv'd fo groffly.

M. BUT yet, you had the pleafure of advancing your friends every day.

G. As feldom as poffible, and did it always unwillingly.

M. HOW then came they to follow you fo much, and almoft adore you as you went along the ftreets?

G. NOW

G. No w 'tis you are catch'd; I am glad to find you so much out, at the knowledge of mankind.

M. Why pray, what is the matter?

G. Obliging men, is not the way to win them.

M. Methinks it should be so.

G. Quite contrary: Every man I advanc'd, thinking his business done, never minded me afterwards; so there I lost a friend, and made a hundred enemies out of envy to him.

M. But yet you order'd your business so, as to have a great many friends, and few enemies, except the *Huguenots.*

G. True: But 'twas only by seeming kind to every body, and all the while caring for nobody. I us'd them just like a herd of beasts, (as indeed they are) encreas'd their number all the ways I could, valu'd them according to their use, but lov'd none. Would you have had me fond of a black Ox, or a red Cow?

M. For ought I see, never man was beloved so much, or deserv'd it so little.

G. Thank you for your complement; and not to be ungrateful, I believe never any Religion has either been spread or practised

3   *so*

fo much as yours, and yet without the leaft fhadow of wit or learning.

M. THAT is the reafon it took fo much. Whoever aims at mankind, muft not fhoot high : fine nets may catch birds, but never hold beafts. Mine were coarfe and ftrong, worth a thoufand of your fchool-diftinctions, which are but flight cobwebs fpun out of eafe and idlenefs. Being witty out of fea-fon, is one fort of folly.

O N

O N

JULIUS CÆSAR.

THAT the lives of famous men are incitements to noble actions, is so vulgar a reflection, that all Prefaces are full of it, and every reader feels it. But in JULIUS CÆSAR, not only when he was at the head of armies, but long before he grew so considerable, there is something so very charming, and so peculiarly remarkable, that I cannot hold from exercising my thoughts on such a noble subject; if it be but to put others in mind, who have more leisure and ability to do it better.

WHEN we read of other Heroes, of ALEXANDER *the Great*, &c. we are more astonish'd than instructed. Perhaps all the circumstances of their story were not so well known; or else the writers of it have done both them and posterity a great deal of wrong, in representing them rather like THESEUS and HERCULES in the fabulous ages,

3 than

than naturally in their own proper colours.
What they are fam'd for, appears methinks
like the Creation of man as defcrib'd by
MOSES; done in an inftant, and we poor
mortals know not how, nor why: With
this difference indeed, that in *Paradife* a
meer human creature was form'd with thofe
failings and imperfections which have been fatal to us ever fince; whereas ALEXANDER, *&c.*
are made fo extraordinary, or rather fo extravagant, and doing things fo impoffible to
human nature, that it ferves no more to our
inftruction than what PLINY writes of flying
Dragons. If this were only an excefs of commendation, the valour of fuch worthies is
great enough to deferve, or at leaft to excufe an hyperbole: But we fee 'tis nothing
befides a meer inclination in the writers to
romance, and extravagance; for, if they
raife them above men in fome places, they
deprefs them as much below beafts in others.
What elfe are the fantaftick unaccountable
vanities, the fottifh debauches, and the in-
human cruelties of ALEXANDER *the Great?*
If you will have my opinion, they are no
more to be credited, than his defending himfelf all alone againft a whole garrifon; where,
if he needlefsly threw himfelf into fuch a
dan-

danger, his valour, great as it was, is scarce sufficient to make amends for his rashness; nor does his force seem more extraordinary than his folly.

But in Cæsar, all appears most naturally becoming, even to his very faults, and imperfections. He is describ'd to us like a a vast tree, tall above the whole grove besides, spreading its branches all about, laden with every sort of delicious fruit: Yet all the while it seems natural, and but a Tree; we see the very seed from whence it grew, and view the daily growth; and observe the winds, that would have often torn it up by the roots, had they not been fixed in the firmest foundation. It bred indeed some cankers within it self: as what in nature is not subject to passions, and infirmities? Yet he stood triumphant even over these, his most dangerous enemies.

Let us begin with his youth, which was so very agreeable, as to please both the husbands and wives at the same time: This I know has been esteem'd rather a blemish to his reputation, by such grave authors as did not rightly consider his character. Indeed this had been unpardonable in Cato a Stoick, and a zealous professor of the most rigorous

ver-

vertue ; but CÆSAR's was above all such narrow rules, like the genius of HOMER in poetry, or of APELLES in painting ; and could never have foar'd fo high, or made fuch lafting flights, without refting it felf fometimes on thefe lower delights of the fenfes. Yet methinks a noblenefs of nature appear'd in his very pleafures, and his ambition of conqueft began with the wives of CRASSUS and POMPEY, the two greateft men in the world at that time ; who, notwithftanding their jealoufy, were fo charm'd by his converfation, that they rais'd him between them to be as confiderable as themfelves ; one by his wealth, the other by his reputation. SERVILIA too muft needs have been the wonder of her age ; for what lefs can we imagine of a woman who was fifter of CATO, mother of BRUTUS, and the beloved miftrefs of JULIUS CÆSAR? Yet all this wandring abroad, did not make him infenfible at home ; for on that difcovery of CLODIUS, he both faid and did the reafonableft thing in the world : he chofe rather to part with his wife, than to keep with her a perpetual anxiety of mind ; and only gave this reafonable account of it, that he could not doubt the vertue of his wife, but much lefs bear the world's having

the

the least fufpicion of it. I was unwilling to mention, among other failings, his extrava-gant fondnefs of CLEOPATRA (if fondnefs of the fineft woman in nature may be call'd extravagant) becaufe it had like to have coft him both life and reputation, and therefore not to be defended. But fince his whole car-riage in *Egypt* appears the greateft and al-moft only error of his whole life; 'tis no little excufe for him, that Love was the only occafion of it. Love, that refiftlefs Paffion! which has forc'd DAVID to contrive a mur-der, SOLOMON to commit idolatry, and all mankink to play the fool at one time or other.

BUT we have been too long intent on his pleafures, as indeed he himfelf was, and fufficiently fenfible of it, when a ftatue of ALEXANDER made him weep; to think a-nother man fhould have almoft conquer'd the world at an age when he had fcarce ap-pear'd in it. The truth is, he was involv'd a-while in debauches, like a fierce Lion in a toil, which his ftrength of mind broke through on the firft occafion that was of-fer'd him by the feveral factions at that time. But I do not mean to write his Life, which has been done fo often and fo well already;

but only to make fome fhort reflections on it, as my memory fhall ferve me ; which can hardly fail of fpringing fome game in fuch an ample field of fame and glory. Firft, The confpiracy of CATILINE prefents us with a-full view of CÆSAR, who was fo violently fufpected to make one in it, that CATO would needs have a Letter open'd publickly in the Senate-houfe, only becaufe it was directed to him : In this furprize he acted with as much prudence, as all the time and advice in the world could have furnifh'd him with. For it happening to be a Love-letter from his dear SERVILIA, and therefore not to be expos'd thus before a company of mo-rofe Senators, who by this accident (one would imagine) muft neceffarily find caufe to cenfure either him, or her, or both, ac-cording to his concealing, or expofing the Letter : Yet CÆSAR in an inftant not only overcame all this difficulty, but reveng'd him-felf on CATO fufficiently, for bringing him into the danger ; who, tho' long before ac-quainted with his fifter's intrigue, was quickly in more confufion than CÆSAR, when he threw him the Letter, and bid him read it publickly, if he durft.

CATO

CATO purſu'd him ſtill, making a moſt violent ſpeech againſt the conſpirators : But CÆSAR, tho' privately one of them, and ſufficiently ſuſpected, yet openly and eloquently defended the reſt, as if they had been only his clients, and not his partners ; and by that firmneſs of mind ſav'd himſelf from the violence of CATO, and the wiles of CICERO, both join'd together to procure his ruine: Yet he was in a manner but an Apprentice in that conſpiracy of CATILINE ; and ſhew'd them ſoon after how much abler he could be than all his maſters, when once he began to ſet up for himſelf ; tho' with a nobler deſign, and in a more generous way ; not to ruine and pillage ſuch a goodly Empire, but improve it in all things, as his more happy ſucceſſors liv'd long enough to accompliſh.

But 'tis high time for us to behold him in the field, where I know the reader expects him with impatience, becauſe that indeed was his proper ſphere ; and never man had ſuch talents for it. His body, notwithſtanding the falling ſickneſs, was ſtrong and active to a wonder, fit for all the exerciſe and fatigues of war ; yet unwieldly and ſluggiſh, in compariſon of his mind, which was rather what

we

we imagine of angelical than humane; such
a ſtrange quickneſs of thought and imagination, join'd with ſo piercing and profound
a judgment; and both ſupported with a
memory and capacity able to do all things
at all times.   *   *   *   *   *   *

UNFINISHED.

THE

THE
STORY
OF
HEROD
AND
Marc Antony,

Collected out of the Roman Historians.

THERE is a passage in the *Roman* History so very remarkable, that it deserves to be more particularly related, with all its circumstances; which, being now at leisure, I have collected out of those several Authors who are reputed the most faithful historians of that time.

Among those many, who, according to the custom of the world, forsook MARC ANTONY in his declining fortune, HEROD was the most considerable; who, though King

N 3

of

of *Judæa* by his particular grace and favour, yet at length was forced to forſake
him; but in ſuch a manner, that all the
world, and even MARC ANTONY himſelf,
could not but acquit him both of meanneſs
and ingratitude. Which ſeems (in my o-
pinion) the plaineſt inſtance, and the higheſt
aggravation of that poor Emperor's imprudence, and infelicity; that his being abandon'd by the very beſt and moſt oblig'd of
all his friends, ſhould be altogether imputed to his own ill conduct, and not to
the leaſt unfaithfulneſs or ingratitude of
HEROD.

HEROD was not allowed the honour of
being at the famous battle of *Actium*; becauſe imployed to finiſh the conqueſt of *A-
rabia*, which ANTONY had privately given
to CLEOPATRA, together with the reverſion
of *Judæa* it ſelf, of which HEROD was
then King. So that ſhe cunningly contrived to ſatisfy her ambition with engaging
HEROD either to gain one Kingdom for her,
or elſe to fall in the attempt, and ſo leave
the other free. But HEROD was not eaſily
impos'd on; and having ended the war in
Arabia ſuccefsfully, brought all the aſſiſtance
of a conqueror to ſupport, if poſſible, the

falling

falling greatnefs of ANTONY. HEROD, it
feems, had long before fufpected the dangerous arts of CLEOPATRA; and like a true
friend, advis'd ANTONY againft her, even in
all the height of her favour and his paffion.
He had prefs'd him efpecially not to carry
her along with him to that unfortunate battle, as if he had forefeen the fatal con-
fequence of her being there. 'Tis no wonder therefore, if he had fome hopes of finding him more prudent at laft by fo fad an
experience; and accordingly made hafte to
overtake him immediately after his over-
throw. There he endeavour'd to raife the
fpirits of his drooping friend, by prefenting him frankly with all the fruits of his
own fuccefs, to ballance in fome meafure
the misfortune of *Actium.* Men, money
and provifions of all forts, he fupplies him
with in abundance; but then takes fo favourable an opportunity to give him the only
advice that could fave him, and at once revenge them both of the falfe CLEOPATRA.
He makes him fenfible that fhe had not only
been his ruine, by her extravagant flight at
the battle of *Actium;* but was now contriving it with AUGUSTUS, the better to prevent her own; to whom fhe had fent a
N 4 trufty

trusty messenger (in the company of A'n-
tony's Ambassadors) who was extremely
well received, while they were refus'd au-
dience. And therefore, unless he were
content to be deliver'd up by CLEOPATRA,
there remained no other course to be taken
but to seize on her, and secure *Ægypt* to
himself; where he might easily make a stand,
'till he was sufficiently recruited to renew
the war. To these most convincing arguments that unfortunate General made only
this reply, after a deep sigh from his very
soul; *I confess*, my friend, *'tis impossible to*
shew at once more friendship, and prudence,
than appears most plainly in the advice you
have now given me; never was a wiser
counsel, nor worse bestow'd; for alas, I am
incapable of following it: And, to make me
throughly unhappy, That love, or rather en-
chantment which ties me yet to CLEOPATRA
as firmly as ever, is not enough to blind me
intirely: For, I see, as well as you, her
falsehood, and consequently my own folly;
but oh! it seems you do not see, as I do, all
those charms that cause it: In a word, I
doat on her to that degree, she may lead me
in chains to CÆSAR, *while I contentedly go*
along gazing on her beauty, and unable to
                                         lose

lose the fight of it, tho' but for a moment. HEROD amaz'd, as much as afflicted, asked him, If it was possible that this could be his final resolution? to which he answer'd only, That it was as unchangeable as fate; and so would have left him, to run immediately into the arms of CLEOPATRA. But HEROD, being a wise man, foresaw now his own ruin every way; for, he was not only sure to fall with MARC ANTONY (which yet he could have almost endur'd patiently for his sake) but to fall by him also, in case some lucky accident of state happen'd to make a turn in his affairs: For who could expect secrecy in such a slave of CLEOPATRA? Or her mercy, after ANTONY had once expos'd him to it? which forc'd HEROD, in spite of all his friendship, to take this last farewel of his unhappy Emperor. *That little assistance which I have brought hither, I am so far from withdrawing again, that I would yet go back to fetch more, if I had not done already all that was possible for me in your service: only my person now I ask your leave to dispose of; and you may judge by this, into what a lost condition your fatal obstinacy has brought us both; since I am forced to leave a Prince I love above all men*

3

living,

living, to try the good nature of one who is remarkable for wanting it, and has already vanquish'd us. ANTONY, as infatuated as he was, yet had generosity enough left, to let him go and seek his own security, and to embrace him at parting with a great deal of tenderness; perhaps having a secret satisfaction in being unloaded of such a friend, who was too true a counsellor not to be sometimes troublesome. HEROD went immediately to *Rhodes,* and presented himself on a sudden before AUGUSTUS CÆSAR. His Diadem indeed was off, but he took care to carry with him all the other marks of regal dignity, with which he appeared rather awful, than submissive; and seem'd more to offer friendship, than to implore favour. Then, after having owned all he had already, and would still have done for ANTONY, if his passion for CLEOPATRA would have suffer'd him to accept his assistance; he at length broke out into this expression. *Think not, oh* OCTAVIUS! *that I quitted* MARC ANTONY, *either out of my own inconstancy, or for that of fortune, which has of late forsaken him. If he would now at last have follow'd my advice, I had freely ventured in his preservation a Kingdom,*
which

which I must acknowledge I owe only to his generofity, and a life, that can never be laid down better than in his fervice. But fince I had not credit enough with that unhappy Man to perfuade him to fave himfelf, I thought it but a foolifh part to fink with any perfon who was bent on his own deftruction; and to remain in a Court, where ANTONY was fo much a flave to CLEOPATRA, that it was impoffible for me to efcape, after the faithful advice I had given againft her. And now here I ftand as much his friend as ever, in my inclinations and wifhes, unlefs you efteem me worthy of being yours; which if you do, I think by all the rules of honour and of gratitude, I am free to follow your fortunes, as heartily as I was before engag'd in his, and am refolv'd to obferve the fame fidelity. AUGUSTUS, who was an admirable judge of all things, embrac'd him with a great deal of refpect, and efteem'd him the more for fo frank a way of proceeding; he procur'd of the Senate to have his Kingdom of *Judæa* confirm'd to him, added to it that of ZENODORUS, and made him his friend ever after.

THIS HEROD was that King of *Judæa* who was counted fo cruel, and not without

out caufe, efpecially to his own family; whom it feems he was exceffively jealous of; which gave occafion for that fharp faying of AUGUSTUS, (notwithftanding their reconcilement,) *That he had rather be* HEROD's *Sow than his Son.* But yet he wanted not fome good qualities to balance his vices, and which juftly gave him the denomination of HEROD *the Great:* Whofe whole proceeding in this matter is the more imitable; becaufe it was univerfally efteem'd in an age, and by a people, the moft fenfible of honour that ever any have been known, within the memory of man.

OBSER-

OBSERVATIONS

ON THE

FIRST BOOK

OF

TULLY's

Epiſtles to ATTICUS.

ADVERTISEMENT.

THIS *is a short Comment on some few passages in* TULLY's *Letters to* ATTICUS, *wherein Monsieur* DE St. REAL *(the best of all the Commentators) is either silent, or else in my opinion a little mistaken; as who is not sometimes?*

BEING at leisure of late, I have amused my self on this subject, because I think these Letters one of the most valuable Pieces of all Antiquity both for use and entertainment; inlarging as well as instructing our minds still more, every time we read them; shining with new beauties, and giving clearer light towards managing the most important affairs.

I.

I must take Notice of a slight touch here and there, in my Notes, on the common Topick of Marriage; which is only to be understood generally, since I am sufficiently satisfied by a most comfortable experience that all such general rules admit of particular exceptions.

OBSER-

OBSERVATIONS on TULLY's
Letters to ATTICUS.

LETTER I.

This was the Fifth Letter in some Editions, but misplaced.

I.

QUANTUM *dolorem,* &c. This very first expression in TULLY's first Letter to ATTICUS, is almost sufficient to recommend all that follows. For 'tis not a meer Affectation of good nature; (such as we

may obferve in the way and words of fome
diffemblers, who yet fhine with it extremely
among thofe who cannot diftinguifh ;) but
this is an appeal to a wife and old acquaintance ; " You who know me fo very well (fays
" CICERO) cannot doubt of my tendernefs
" at the lofs of my kinfman." If we had not
ftill remaining a great many other inftances of
his good nature ; yet this fingle expreffion of
his, would have left us fome idea of it.
Which I take the more notice of, becaufe he
was the fharpeft ill-natured Orator in all *Rome*,
againft thofe who indangered her Liberty :
That eager inveteracy in behalf of his native
Country, was it feems no way inconfiftent
with the moft gentle and affable temper we
know of, among all the *Romans*.

THAT which follows in this Letter, fhews
he did not bewail his lofs without caufe ; for
he gives his kinfman in a few words the fineft
character imaginable. " Agreeable in con-
" verfation, and ufeful both in publick and
" private affairs." Such an unaffected commendation from fo great a judge, is more
valuable than a hundred monuments and
panegyricks.

II.

II.

QUOD *ad me scribis de sorore,* &c. This is another instance of his good disposition, in taking such pains to dissuade a married couple from living together uneasily ; a business hard enough to bring about with all his eloquence. Yet I should not have taken notice of it, but for his great politeness in the way of such an interposition : mixing the authority of an elder brother, the head of his house, with the freedom of a familiar and affectionate friend. For 'tis no easy matter in the exercise of authority, to be neither remiss, nor haughtily imperious.

III.

QUOD *scribis, etiam si,* &c. This reconcilement which TULLY was to make between ATTICUS and LUCCEIUS (for that we find afterward to be his name) is mightily taken notice of in a little *French* book call'd CESARION : wherein the author, tho' very wittily, seems a little over-fond of a paradox he maintains against the celebrated character of ATTICUS ; of whose failings in friendship he quotes this very quarrel for one instance, yet without understanding what was the oc-

casion

cafion of it.   'Tis a little odd too in that author, to conclude ATTICUS guilty of breach
of friendfhip, only becaufe earneft to renew
it; and LUCCEIUS innocent, becaufe implacable.   And, fince that Gentleman affects
fingularity in his difcourfes, I think he could
hardly have fhewn a plainer inftance of it.
I cannot but take notice of one expreffion in
ATTICUS's Letter, which CICERO repeats in
this; " You write (fays he) that if any body
" be your enemy, 'tis my bufinefs to appeafe
" him."   Friendfhip muft have run pretty
high in an age when fuch an expreffion was
proper : and the moft accomplifh'd Gentleman of all *Rome* would hardly have ufed it
to one of the greateft, if his own heart and
active affection had not been warm enough
to warrant fuch an expectation of a fuitable
return.   Which he met with accordingly;
fince CICERO here owns the right of fervice
he claims of him; and feveral letters fhew his
punctual performance of it, tho' unfuccefs-
fully.   For it feems it was eafier for CICERO
to perfuade whole Senates and popular Affemblies, than one obftinate, though moft
eftimable perfon, as LUCCEIUS appears to be
in all the accounts we have of him.   Which
is lefs to be wondred at, becaufe thofe are two
very

very different Talents, publick eloquence, and private infinuation.

IV.

E x *omnibus moleſtiis*, &c. This ſeems to me a little ſtrange in TULLY, the moſt eaſy-humoured, and facetious man in the world; whoſe very great genius was ſo fit alſo for buſineſs, that methinks he ſhould not be ſo tired with it, as never to be at eaſe except in his Library. Yet juſt at that time perhaps ſome unuſual affairs crouded upon him, of no great moment to the publick; for had that been concern'd, I am confident he would never have grudg'd his pains, but made it rather his greateſt pleaſure. I impute all this complaint to his uſual good breeding in making that an excuſe, for thoſe many repeated troubles he gave ATTICUS about trifles towards adorning his Library; which therefore he profeſſes here to be his only ſatisfaction. If it be objected that an excuſe has an air of ceremony, which is not only formal, but faulty among friends: it may be obſerv'd, he makes no difficulty of imploying ATTI-cus often on this occaſion, and only ſhews a little politeneſs in pretending it was now grown his only ſatisfaction; that ſo his

friend

friend might have the more, in gratifying that humour.

V.

Cujus *sermonis genus*, &c. This impertinent conversation of ACUTILIUS puts us in mind of a great many, who, though far from being silly in managing their own private affairs, are yet in conversation worse to be endur'd than an ordinary Fit of the cholick : Accordingly CICERO puts it down here pleasantly, as the greatest uneasiness his friendship had ever made him undergo, to have been so long in such tedious company upon his account.

LETTER II.

In some Editions this was the Sixth, but mistaken.

QUID *agas*, &c. This is one of the pleasures, as well as privileges of friendship. *Rome* was the place in all the world of the greatest affairs, and of the most entertainment : TULLY was one of the busiest men in it ; yet amidst all this, he inquires with

with earneftnefs about every little thing his friend not only does, but thinks, and intends to do. Though I am apt to believe there was fomething of his own natural vivacity in the cafe ; whofe active mind, and capacioufnefs of thought, the whole Empire of *Rome* was fcarce large enough to imploy fufficiently : So vaft a thing is the mind of fome men. Which I fay not altogether by way of commendation, but of admiration rather ; for wherever it is fuch, there appears fomething of rambling, as well as reafoning, in fo great a genius.

LETTER III.

In fome Editions this was made a Part of the laft Letter, I fuppofe for its fhortnefs only ; fince it is plainly a different Letter.

OMNEM *fpem delectationis,* &c. Here he repeats again his great expectation of pleafure in the Library he was now contriving ; which I fhould not take notice of, but upon account of that time of life for which he defign'd it, *Cum in otium venerimus ;* This is one fign how mnch CICERO

was

was fitted by nature, for learning, as well as publick business; because he seems ever preparing himself to retire out of it; and as capable in his closet to divert himself, or instruct the world, as he was in the *Forum* or Senate-house to govern it. This is no small advantage in Republicks, where a sort of rotation is necessary, by which men are seen under several capacities, and much better judg'd of in such different lights, than in a Monarchy; where one man chuses either among those few commended to him by their friends, or among others disguised always by their own insinuations and flattery.

LETTER IV.

HERMÆ *tui pentelici*, &c. I am heartily glad to find this fondness of Statues, *&c.* in such a man as CICERO; though I am not surprized at it, because I scarce ever knew or read of any great genius insensible of such things: For indeed they have a real value in themselves, and not only (as some imagine) in the fancy of Virtuosoes.

LET.

L E T T E R V.

I.

NIMIUM *raro nobis,* &c. On this occasion the ingenious Author of the best notes upon these Letters, admires very justly at the want of *Posts* in such an Empire as the *Roman;* especially considering that CYRUS had in some measure established them above four hundred years before. But I cannot understand how these words shew any such deficiency; because a Post-office had been of no use to so important a correspondence as this, which certainly deserved the care of particular expresses, and all the secrecy imaginable. A method easier among them, by reason of their multitude of slaves, ready, and generally very faithful on all occasions.

II.

ET *Arcæ nostræ confidito,* &c. Here TULLY is so wise, as not to spare his purse for his pleasure; and seems overjoyed to feel a new taste of Statues and such curiosities coming upon him : Knowing a fresh appetite,

tite, at his Age, to be the moſt deſirable jewel that a rich man can poſſibly purchaſe.

LETTER VI.

From Tuſculum, CICERO's *Country-houſe,* *to* ATTICUS *at* Athens.

CUM *eſſem in Ceramico,* &c. Here is a ſmall touch of that agreeable raillery, in which the *Romans,* and among them our author moſt particularly excelled. ATTICUS, it ſeems, had dated his laſt Letter from a famous place in *Greece ;* CICERO therefore, who could not in this anſwer to it affix ſo ſtately a name on the top, and yet had the vanity (which was his Foible) to be willingly out-done by no-body ; falls a raillying of him in revenge, as if he ſuppoſed ATTICUS had affected to write from ſuch a celebrated city ; and ſo as formally dates his Letter in this manner, *From* Tuſculum, CICERO's *Country Seat, to* ATTICUS *at* Athens. Theſe two places are now indeed almoſt equally famous on account of CICERO, and on the ſame account of having been once inhabited by the nobleſt defenders of Liberty, in the

two

two moſt glorious Commonwealths that ever were.

II.

MAGNOPERE *confido illum*, &c. This is an inſtance of that human frailty, which bears ſo great a part in the very wiſeſt minds. Here CICERO undertakes the reconcilement of LUCCEIUS to his beloved ATTICUS, with all the alacrity and ardour of a true and an induſtrious friend : But at the ſame time ſhews too great a confidence in himſelf of the ſucceſs (as indeed vanity was his only Foible) not conſidering, that Eloquence is more capable of turning a whole aſſembly of Senators, than of convincing one angry or obſtinate perſon. And accordingly it prov'd ſo in this caſe. For, beſides that TULLY's way of reaſoning was rather agreeable and florid, than ſtrong and nervous; no man accuſtomed to great aſſemblies, finds his imagination ſo lively, or his underſtanding ſo large in any dry converſation of buſineſs, as when warm'd in publick with hopes of applauſe, and of ſerving his Country; in both which CICERO uſed to ſucceed ſo gloriouſly. I have often obſerv'd this difference at Committees of Parliament, and Cabinet-Councils;

Councils; where men would speak well, and even with warmth sometimes; but seldom with so much force and eloquence, as in a full House of Parliament.

III.

SIGNA *nostra*, &c. He had owned in a former Letter, how much Statues and such curiosities for setting off his Library, were become his principal inclination: and it appears plainly by so many unnecessary repetitions of it. Which I take notice of, only as a warning to my self and others, that we may be so watchful over our eagerness and impatience, as never to let it trouble our friends, though perhaps we cannot help being unquiet with it our selves.

IV.

NON *minimum quod soror prægnans est.* I wonder he mentions his Sister-in-law's being with child, as no little proof of his brother's kindness; which yet sure is none of the greatest, unless TULLY thought it hard to lie with a man's own wife, as perhaps he found it with TERENTIA.

V.

V.

DE *comitiis meis,* &c. Here is, in one instance, more good nature, and good breeding, (two of the best qualities any man can have) than now appears in a whole age among us; and therefore it deserves a little explanation. CICERO had a pretension to the Pretorship, in which nothing could be more useful than ATTICUS's presence at *Rome,* one of the most considerable and popular men in it. Yet TULLY not only, to prevent his trouble in making such a journey, dispenses with his absence, but furnishes him with the best excuses in the world for it. " Because (says he) I am more concern'd in " whatever you are transacting of greater " importance for your self at *Athens,* than " for any affairs of my own in *Rome.*" And what is yet more than this, because CICERO knew the niceness of his temper, which would not hazard the being reproached for neglecting his friend at such a time; he not only very positively forbids him to take the journey, but assures him all their friends shall know as much; that in case he lose the Pretorship by his absence, the blame may only fall upon himself for it. I know not how
the

the reader will be affected at this, but I want words to express my own sense of so friendly and so noble a proceeding : and that which heightens it, is the wonderful ambition among the *Romans* of arriving early at these great imployments, so as sometimes to kill themselves upon having failed of their pretension; add also the particular eagerness of TULLY's humour for all things he desired, (as we saw just now) but especially for honours and preferments, even to excess. Yet how frankly, how generously does he sacrifice all this, only to ease his friend of a troublesome journey! Such a man was CICERO; and such a place was *Rome*, which had many CICEROES! Men not only like him, but even above him with all his parts and politeness. And yet we have the farce sometimes of hearing ignorant wretches, especially the *French*, undervalue both *Greeks* and *Romans*, in comparison with themselves.

LETTER VII.

I.

V ERUM *ne caufam quidem*, &c. It seems this quarrel between ATTICUS and LUCCEIUS (for that appears to be his name)

I

name) was very hearty on one fide; for nothing fhews that more than fuch an obftinate denial to declare the true caufe of it; tho' 'tis alfo a fign of being implacable, and revengeful. In which I differ with the Abbot of St. REAL, who, after affirming rightly that, *Les plus grands & les plus fenfibles fujets de plainte fe difent le moins,* is yet methinks a little miftaken in judging fuch a fullen filence reafonable, notwithftanding all interpofition of friends. But I fee, no fort of good fortune is without allay; for ATTICUS, fo particularly famous for living not only inoffenfively, but almoft friendlily with all Men; has yet fome way or other provoked two implacable enemies, this LUCCEIUS of old, and our ingenious Abbot now; who, befides his notes on thefe Letters between ATTICUS and CICERO, has in a little book called *Cæfarion,* ufed the firft of them almoft as unmercifully as ANTONY did the other: So that I am confident if our Author had lived in thofe times, and if private combats had been then in fafhion, (which are two *If's,* I confefs, as far fetch'd as fome of his reflections) he would have been LUCCEIUS's fecond, and perhaps have fought a duel with CICERO.

II.

II.

SUMMUM *me eorum studium tenet,* &c. There can hardly be a greater proof than this of the ravishing delights of Learning. That such a man as CICERO, whose agreeable sort of wit so fitted him for the pleasures of conversation, and whose great talents help'd him to all the satisfaction his ambitious humour was capable of; yet to his intimate friend he makes a solemn protestation of being no where so well pleas'd as among his Books and Papers. But, to his immortal honour, it ought to be observed also, that, notwithstanding all his inclination to Philosophy, and ability of instructing the world that way, yet he always prefer'd doing well, to writing well, and sacrificed his own humour [the most difficult self-denial, because a continual one] to the publick service, and the safety of his country : For which his great concern at this time, seeing affairs so ill managed, drew from him this expression of fondness for his Library, that now afforded him his only consolation.

L E T-

LETTER VIII.

A VIAM *tuam,* &c. I hope this Grand-mother of ATTICUS was some impertinent old Dotard; for otherwise, CICERO acquaints him with her death methinks a little too flightingly. But his raillery upon her Bigotry does something excuse it self, by mentioning so good a reason for his undervaluing her, and even jesting on her death. Which I can never impute to the manners of those times, as ST. REAL does; because I should think their being more refin'd than we are, should rather incline them to more good nature, and greater respect to Parents. I must differ also with him again about the consolatory Letter which CICERO jestingly supposes that SAUFEIUS (an *Epicurean* friend of theirs) would write to ATTICUS on this occasion. SAUFEIUS (says he) believing death to be no harm, nor any thing after it, was found out pleasantly by CICERO for that condoling office, as one who could be troubled at nothing; if that had been TULLY's meaning, he would rather have chosen some *Stoick* for the purpose; whereas the *Epicu-*

reans, tho' turning every ill accident to the beſt uſe (as all wiſe men do) yet own'd a tender ſenſe of both pain and pleaſure ; ſo that I fancy rather he pick'd him out for his ſoftneſs ; which, ſhewn on this occaſion, would have appear'd indeed ſufficiently ridiculous. After all, this is but gueſſing at random ; and I ſhould be loth to be earneſt in trifles, or wrangle about the meaning of a Letter written ſeventeen hundred years ago ; as our Criticks ſometimes do with the ſame concern as if it were about the words of a *Will*, on which their whole eſtates depended.

LETTER IX.

I.

NOS *hic incredibilis*, &c. Here appears a right diſpoſition of mind for a perſon in publick buſineſs : To regard in the firſt place the doing of juſtice, and yet to enjoy very great ſatisfaction in that applauſe which attends it ; For ſure it is allowable in Morality, as well as Divinity, to look up to the rewards expected. The truth is, the love of Vertue and of Fame moſt commonly go together ;

gether; and no doubt are made to do so for
encouragement to Vertue, by the wisdom of
that Being which has contrived all things.

II.

QUOD *ad me de Hermathena scribis,* &c.
'Tis impossible to shew more eager fondness
for Statues and Books, than appears every
where in these Letters : Though perhaps the
first was principally for the sake of the last,
since they were to stand in his Library ; a
place to which he had so violent an inclination, as to make him mention it always in
the hyperbolical style of a very Lover.

LETTER X.

ABS *te peto ut mihi hoc ignoscas,* &c.
Here he puts gratitude (and I love him
for it) as the best reason in the world for refusing any body, and indeed for doing any
thing. But when he mentions ambition as
another excuse, methinks he needed a much
greater apology, and to use all his rhetorick
for denying so faithful a friend.

P 2　　　　　　　　LET-

LETTER *to* POMPEY.

NULLA *enim re tam lætari soleo*, &c. CICERO here appears such an honest man, and of so noble a nature, that 'tis impossible not to be touched with it. A good action, says he, rewards itself, and all your ingratitude cannot make me the least repent of it, or deprive me of a very great satisfaction in having done my part of friendship, even at this time while I am thus reproaching the failure of yours.

IF I wou'd strain some excuse for being ungrateful (of which it stands sufficiently in need) it shou'd be this great satisfaction of mind in doing any generous well-natur'd action; the pleasure of which pays itself abundantly, without needing any reward or return. Here also, TULLY shews himself a master in the mystery of politicks, by warning POMPEY against courting his enemies, instead of indulging his friends; which is the way only to be despised by both: The quite contrary practice being the surest means both of rising high, and standing firm.

LET.

LETTER *to* METELLUS CELER.

EGO *dolori tuo non solum ignosco,* &c. I know not what effect it will have on others, but I am enamour'd of this candid temper of CICERO, in not only pardoning the unreasonable anger of METELLUS, in behalf of his brother; but confessing what a softness he felt to his near relations on the like occasions; and how much that experience inclined him to allow it the better in another man, though now it happened to be against himself. What gentleness! what prudence! how just an indulgence to the weakness of human nature.

LETTER XIII.

CONSUL *autem ipse,* &c. An admirable picture in a few words! Perhaps as sharp a censure as was ever written, and deserving a very particular notice, by all lovers of either Eloquence or Satire.

TANTUM *quod ea emptione,* &c. Upon this occasion there is no denying that TULLY

P 3

once

once broke the Law, in borrowing money
of a criminal he defended, in order to finifh
a great houfe he was building : I am heartily forry for it, and would give money to
be able to defend him.   I can only excufe
him a little, by remarking, that it was not
by a thoufand parts fo bad an action, as if
he had for lucre accufed an innocent ; and
hope for his fake, that the temptation did
not lie in the money, but only in his great
impatience for building ; being the moft
eager man in the world for any thing of
that kind.

LETTER XIV.

EGO *autem ipfe, Dii boni !* &c. Once
for all, this conftant appearance of
vanity in fo great and wife a man, deferves
fome particular reflection, a little beyond
the vulgar manner of commentators : It
having been always made fo great an objection to that excellent perfon, the rather
I believe, becaufe indeed they cou'd find no
other to make. Firft, nothing is more plain
and reafonable in judging of the antients,
than to make allowance both for times and
places :

places: without which, how extravagant will CATO feem, in making no more of lending his wife, than we do now-a-days in fparing a friend fome rare ambler for a journey of pleafure. Nay, what fhall we think of the two wives of JACOB, for kindly affording him a couple of handfome Handmaids? The *Romans* were naturally extremely vain-glorious, and politickly encouraged that humour in every body, as being a conftant inciter to virtue, and all forts of noble actions. Religion alfo was concern'd in it; fince fame and reputation cannot but imply a future ftate; the prefent here being of too fmall extent to be temptation enough for venturing all things to acquire it; efpecially in lofing even Life itfelf fo frankly, without a firm belief of having amends made them hereafter, in that to come.

AFTER all, no man can be further than I am from making this the leaft excufe for vanity now-a-days; for in behalf of TULLY himfelf, I can find none fufficient, except from the age and country he liv'd in. In ours, I believe, there is nothing will more keep down a man's reputation than his own eagernefs, and therefore fillinefs, in openly

P 4

taking

taking notice of it. But the circumstances were otherwise with CICERO ; who yet sometimes cou'd not hold from rallying himself about it. All this while too, I have said nothing of his being unable with all his Eloquence, to speak greater things of himself, than History speaks of him, and than all his Writings speak for him.

Left Unfinished.

THE

THE
LETTER
OF
EPICURUS
TO
MENECEUS.

THE youngest persons should not defer reflecting on vertue and morality, nor the oldest give over weary of it; for who is either too young, or too old, to keep his mind as easy as 'tis possible? Youth will by practice of this grow wiser and happier every day; and old age itself may, by such a help, enjoy over-again in some measure the soft hours of youth; by avoiding all anxious thoughts, not only of the future, but the present. Apply your self therefore, oh MENECEUS, to follow my advice, with an assurance that all these things are the very principles of happiness.

BE-

BELIEVING then, firſt, that GOD or the original cauſe of all things, is ſomething immortal and happy, which the light of nature informs us ; be tender of attributing with the vulgar, to that glorious Being, any thing that is in the leaſt repugnant to its divine nature.

THERE are alſo other inviſible ſubſtances ; but not ſuch as men imagine to themſelves, and deſcribe yet otherwiſe than they imagine, when they preach about it. He therefore who denies the common opinions of the people, is not impious ; but he who maintains them : for ſuch idle notions come not from the light of reaſon, but from meer fear and fancy. They believe rightly, that the Gods puniſh the wicked and reward the good ; but then 'tis only becauſe they themſelves wou'd do ſo, and therefore they think thoſe ſuperior Beings of juſt the ſame humour ; by which ſcanty meaſure they judge of all things.

ACCUSTOM yourſelf to think death of no concern to us, ſince all pleaſure and pain depends on our ſenſes, and death is nothing but an utter deprivation of them all.

A firm Aſſurance that death is nothing more, is the only way to make life eaſy ; without vain hopes on one hand, or anxious

fears

fears on the other. While we are alive, death is abfent; and when death comes, we are fo: Therefore, fince it does no harm, who but a fool wou'd fear it? Even life is good, not according to its length, but as we pafs it in quiet and fatisfaction.

'Tis equally needlefs to advife the young to live, or the old to die; for as Life is amiable to the one, death is as neceffary to the other, and the reafon is the fame for both. Whoever talks of wifhing not to have been born, is ridiculous; becaufe, if in earneft, why does he not kill himfelf? and, if in jeft, none but a fool would make that a laughing matter.

We ought to think the future fo much ours only, as that it may come; but not depend on it, as if it muft do fo.

We all have defires, of which fome are natural and ufeful; others are not fo; of the natural, fome are more neceffary than others: The neceffary are partly for life itfelf; and the reft, for the eafe and pleafure of it. The plain knowledge of this will make us fee what we ought to follow, or avoid, either for health of body, or repofe of mind; which two things compleat our happinefs. The attaining of thefe is all we have to do; for Pleafure is only the fenfe of fupplying fome want; and therefore when we feel none of any kind, there is nothing to wish, or desire.

THIS is the reason of our maintaining Pleasure to be the only principle of Happiness; because every body feels 'tis the first gift of nature, at our coming into the world; as 'tis the last with which we go out of it. It must certainly be the measure of all good; and if we sometimes chuse pain, or trouble before it, 'tis always in order to some greater satisfaction afterward: Therefore all pleasure is not so good, as that we should blindly abandon ourselves to it, no more than always avoid trouble; but only weigh both, and on occasion serve ourselves of either.

I count temperance and self-denial a great vertue; not that we should generally practise it; but only sometimes, that we may the better endure any want which may happen to us, As none act well in great stations, but such as value them but a little.

WE must know also, that whatever is necessary to our nature, is to be had easily; and what is difficult to come by, may as easily be spared. The coarsest fare will give full pleasure to a man who is hungry; and since only bread and water will delight in necessity, 'tis good to fast often; for abstinence

is

is the great preferver of health and vigour ; befides that it makes us much more fenfible of delicacies.

By this time it is plain enough, that when I eftablifh pleafures as our chiefeft good, I am far from meaning thofe only of the lazy and luxurious, who look no farther than fenfual ones : And yet the ignorant are apt to mif-interpret us.   All my aim is, with the ut-moft art and care, to avoid uneafinefs either of mind or body.   'Tis not pleafures and di-verfions, delicacies of diet or other things, nor even the joys of women, that can make a Life intirely happy, tho' fome of thefe may be good ingredients to it ; but only good fenfe and temperance, with a rational inquiry into the nature of things, fo as to be throughly difengag'd from all thofe vulgar errors which fo much difquiet the greateft part of man-kind.

The principle of all thefe things, and therefore our fovereign good, is nothing but Prudence ; which accordingly deferves to be valu'd above all Learning and Philofophy ; becaufe all other vertues proceed from this vertue alone, which firft convinces us that we ought to defire the reft, and then affifts us in the obtaining them.

Pru-

PRUDENCE shews us there is no living comfortably, without obferving juftice and honour in all our actions : And thus vertue and pleafure do not only confift together, but are indeed infeparable.

THESE things fuppofed, what man can go higher than he, who has reverend thoughts of the fupreme Caufe? is without apprehenfion either of death, or of what comes after it? who underftands fo well the nature of man, and his chief felicity, as to believe it eafily attainable; and that all pain is either fhort, or to be indured with patience : fo finds to his comfort, that not a fatal neceffity, (the melancholy doctrine of the Stoicks) but his own free-will, is the only power on which his happinefs depends; and therefore, fince left to himfelf, his good actions will deferve praife, and his ill ones no excufe. For 'tis fafer to go along with the crowd in all their fuperftitions, than inflave one's felf to that tyrant, Deftiny; becaufe the firft, as foolifh as it is, will only miflead us fometimes with vain hopes of favour from the Deity, in return of our obfequious applications to him; but the other is inflexible and inexorable.

How-

HOWEVER, take care of falling into the contrary extream, by making fortune a deity, as the foolish people fancy; for divine power does nothing irregular, or inconstantly. But prefer the greatest misfortune undeserved, to any advantage whatsoever that comes by injuftice.

REFLECT then on these things night and day; alone, and in company of the same disposition; fo, whether you sleep or wake, all will go easy (for even dreams partake of our daily amusements, and depend on temper) and you will live among men almost like a better fort of being: for he that passes his life in possession of these divine truths, with intire felicity, is scarce to be reckoned a humane creature.

ESSAYS.

ESSAYS

ON

FRIENDSHIP.

I AM apt to think Friendſhip a kind of Science ; not that inclination is unneceſſary in the caſe, but 'tis as neceſſary to cultivate it with a great deal of care. That which confirms me in the opinion of its being a Science, is my obſerving it to be almoſt abſolutely loſt, there remaining hardly a ſhadow of it now-a-days : for ſure Nature would not decay, but is much the ſame in all ages.

My Lord Chancellor Bacon obſerves very juſtly, that we now ſee nothing of it between Equals ; and only a little of it ſometimes where the different degrees of men render each of them uſeful and neceſſary to the other : As between a wealthy country-gentleman and his led-captain, or rather his fellow-drunkard ; between a great courtier and one of his dependant flatterers ; whereas inequality is quite contrary to the very na-

Q 2

ture

ture of Friendfhip, which like Love, either finds people equal, or makes them fo.

THEREFORE as that advice is now-a-days thought very wife, of trufting friends with fuch a referve as may preferve us from them, when turn'd enemies; 'tis only becaufe we fuppofe no real friends in fo corrupt an age: for with true friendfhip that doctrine is inconfiftent. And indeed (comparing the very beft fort now, with both the precepts and examples of former times) Friendfhip is not the fame thing which CICERO, and even MONTAGN fo lately defcribe it; and whatever the firft of thofe was, the latter is certainly a moft fincere writer: For a judicious reader may be as fure of MONTAGN's fincerity, as skilful artifts are of a picture's being done by the Life, when there are fuch natural and lively touches in it, as no man's fancy in the world can reach. But to return to friendfhip, I cannot prefume to advife any thing; but out of fome experience I have had in Courts, I think it fafer to depend on thofe who have oblig'd us, than on thofe whom we have oblig'd, though never fo much.

WHENCE fhou'd this ftrange paradox proceed? If it were not too common every day, an ungrateful perfon wou'd appear a

greater

greater monfter, than any man with three legs or four hands.

THIS fure, like moft other faults of human nature, proceeds from Pride, which makes us afham'd of our debts even to friends, and fhun the very remembrance: It makes indeed a little amends, by inciting us to oblige people fometimes, only that they may be in our debt; for I am confident, that of ten courtefies now received, there are fcarce two beftowed out of meer good nature or friendfhip: and to fay truth, they are moft commonly returned accordingly. Yet that is but an ill excufe for ingratitude, which indeed admits of none: For by this argument, a Son would owe nothing to his Father, becaufe he begot him only for his pleafure, and the child came out by the bye: there would be yet a greater pleafure in unbegetting fuch a Son, if poffible.

ONE of the reafons why our Tragedies now are fo little to be valued in comparifon with thofe of the Ancients, is our changing this noble and almoft divine fubject of Friendfhip for foft effeminate Love-matters: For though Love and Friendfhip are equally tender and touching, yet the former of thefe is

Q 3   not

not ſo heroick, or ſo capable of great thoughts and actions.

To conclude: The Friendſhip we read of in former ages, was a noble union of two worthy perſons ſtriving to out-do each other in all kind of good offices, without the leaſt interruption to the very cloſe of their lives, which therefore always end with honour and reputation.

O N

ON
PHILOSOPHY.

NO body has more veneration than my felf for the old Philofophers: I believe human Wit is incapable of reaching higher than PYTHAGORAS, DE- MOCRITUS, PLATO, and ARISTOTLE, or even GASSENDUS and DESCARTES in our days : and therefore 'tis great pity they aim'd at fuch fort of things as are never to be reached. SOCRATES therefore feems the wifeft of them all, not purely on account of his modefty, but becaufe he apply'd himfelf only to Mo- rality, certainly the moft ufeful of all ftu- dies: whereas the fpeculations of the reft, though never fo ingenioufly imagin'd or a- greeably exprefs'd, are yet little better in reality than meer Romances, finely contrived and made to cohere well together, mixed

Q 4

with

with a vaſt deal of wit and fancy. But oh, how deſpicable is the folly of mankind, if this be all the wiſdom of it! If PLATO and ARISTOTLE were no wiſer than to fix and imploy their minds on empty fancies, what ſilly creatures are the common ſort of men? If thoſe of the greateſt wit and judgment imaginable could ſpend all their time in gravely conſidering if the world had a beginning or not; and if it had, whether it came from accident or providence; and write whole books on ſuch ſort of ſubjects: 'tis a manifeſt proof, that the very beſt a man is able to do is only *inſanire cum ratione*. All theſe inquiries, though made by the ableſt Philoſophers, are juſt as if a man, who cannot read a word without ſpectacles, ſhould yet pretend without them to ſee, and ſhew us what they are doing in the Moon.

YET, I will allow ſuch high ſpeculations are pretty ſubjects for our thoughts and fancies, and to improve them alſo; as boys throwing ſtones at birds, will ſtrengthen their arms though they never hit any.

ALL this conſider'd; methinks, of the ſeveral Philoſophers, the *Scepticks* appear the moſt reaſonable, becauſe the leaſt poſitive: As at *Bedlam*, among ſuch a variety of of humours, if we faw one of them chide the reft for being fo noify and violent, fufpecting their infirmity as well as his own; fhould we not think him much the beft of them, and rather too fober for the reft of his companions? The *Dogmatifts* object to this, that even *Scepticks* are as pofitive in denying the knowledge of things, as others are in the maintaining it. But I think they do them wrong; for the *Scepticks* only remain in doubt of all things, which they find themfelves and all mankind befides unable to comprehend.

THE truth of the matter is; all this weaknefs even of thofe wifeft men proceeds from the vanity of believing human nature capable of underftanding all things: And becaufe a Man has that troublefome faculty of amufing, and even tormenting himfelf fometimes with thoughts of a thoufand matters which he has nothing to do with; he is prefently apt to believe them all within his comprehenfion. Whereas a man is no more a creature fit to find out fuch abftrufe matters, than a fifh is made to play a game at bowles. Yet I would not be underftood to difcourage, or the leaft undervalue Learning, where it tends to any manner of ufefulnefs: only to bridle

a

a little that arrogant humour of imagining
our felves capable of knowing the greateſt
matters, when all the while we ſcarce underſtand the very ſmalleſt.

O N

ON
VANITY.

I AM endeavouring on all occasions that happen in conversation, to depress that foolish pride of human nature, which makes us so apt to over-value our selves, as well as to despise all other creatures: And I grow from every dispute more confirm'd in my own opinion, by the ignorance and conceitedness I meet with in those who contradict it.

IF we could imagine a pack of hounds extremely despising the huntsmen, and firmly believing all that noise and clutter was only intended by providence to make sport for a few dogs; the men (I suppose) would think them as ridiculous animals, as I do now the huntsmen for the same reason. Therefore, in my opinion, none of their old definitions of a rational animal, or a laughing animal, expresses the peculiar nature of man half so rightly, as that of a vain animal. For though most

moſt deſpicable creatures our ſelves, yet we
go ſtalking up and down deſpiſing all the
creation beſides, and fancy it was made only
for our ſakes : which is a ſottiſh ſort of arrogance, that no other creature in the world
beſides appears to be guilty of.

YET while I thus blame others, it occurs
to my memory what PLATO ſo wittily reply'd to DIOGENES, trampling with his dirty
feet on one of his embroider'd couches, and
crying out, *Thus I trample on the pride of*
PLATO ; who only ſhook his head, ſaying,
But with more pride thou do'ſt it, good
DIOGENES.　For I am more jealous of it in
my ſelf than in any body elſe, knowing how
little excuſe I have for it.

O N

ON
CRITICISM.

THERE have been always Criticks; and some few good, among a great many bad ones; but I believe there was never such an age and nation for that humour as ours is at present. In so great a town as *London*, there is always a little of the Plague in some odd corner or other; but sometimes 'tis epidemical, and sweeps all away. Just so 'tis now with Criticism, which without the least distinction spares nobody. That I mean, which is vented in eating-houses, coffee-houses, and play-houses; and is nothing in the world but a mixture of ill-nature and ignorance. But, the worst is, these bleak winds are ever blasting all our hopeful blossoms; for they hinder the modesteft and best wits from writing; but, like winds too, they can hardly hurt what is well ripened, and come forth: For 'tis almost in-

3   fallible

fallible that a real good thing will bear out it felf, and in a little time get the better of all oppofition. Time therefore, in all matters of writing, is the only true touchftone of merit; which at length will prevail over all the folly and faction imaginable.

. As in old *Rome*, what made fuch excellent orators above any fince, but the univerfal endeavour of all mankind then to be eloquent? So here, among fo many Cricks, 'tis impoffible but fome few muft be fitted by nature for fuch an exact judgment of things; and it being fo much the fafhion, they cannot fail by art and practice to improve their talent.

THE bufinefs of a Critick is mightily miftaken among us; for our Town-fparks think it confifts in nothing but finding fault, which is but the leaft half of their work. Every man who drinks his pot, can judge a paultry picture in an alehoufe to be worth nothing; but how few can difcern the beft touches, and judge of a good collection!

'TIS furely not undecent to mention one's felf, when 'tis rather with cenfure than approbation. When I came firft abroad into the world, being extremely young, I thought it a fine thing to laugh at every body, to

3   fhew

fhew my wit ; and fancied my felf the better, as I reprefented others to be worfe : but
now I defpife that affectation, which is as ridiculous, as if a Lady would fweep out the
naftinefs of a room, to fhew her own neat-
nefs. Let the half-wits do it, 'tis their drudgery.

I confefs I am ftill very difficult in matters of writing, and feldom find any thing
worth commending, becaufe of thofe great
Idea's I have of the Antients : which make
me yet more unfatisfied with my felf than
with any body elfe. But when I meet with
any thing that deferves it, I approve it gladly,
both for the juftice of the thing, and becaufe
I give fome proof of my own candour and
eafinefs of humour, which (without partiality)
hath nothing of the envy fo common now-
a-days even among our beft wits. Yet perhaps this may proceed from a fort of vanity,
of which I am as apt to fufpect my felf
guilty, as any body ; knowing fo well that
all fort of writers, efpecially Poets, are too
much inclined to it.

A n ill Critick is, I think, of all forts of
writers the moft contemptible ; a very fop
of a Wit. Yet fuch as Wo--y, &c. are even
below that. They are no better than little
dogs that bark at a traveller ; if he be fuch

a

a fool to ſtop his journey, or ſo much as ſlaſh his whip at them, he'll draw on more noiſe, and the boys of the town to boot; but if he rides on his way, the poor Curs ſneak away home, and are no more taken notice of.

O N

O N
AUTHORS.

'TIS a ftrange thing to obferve how very wifely and morally fome men will write, and yet all the while live almoft like the vulgar; as TULLY of old, and of late my Lord BACON; both, I believe, of as great parts and knowledge as ever any age has produced.

THEY differ in many things, but in this they are alike; in having written fo very philofophically, and almoft divinely on all manner of fubjects, efpecially morality: Yet the firft was too great a flatterer of an Ufurper, his Country's Tyrant, extolling him every where againft his very confcience; as appears by his railing at him as much after his death, and grieving that he had no hand in it. Alfo no man was fo extremely fenfible of any turn of fortune; a fign of a little fpirit, confidering the magnanimous temper of thofe times.

VOL. II.   R   He

He expos'd alſo his vanity a little too much even for thoſe times, when it was moſt in faſhion ; and indeed it was a wiſe mode, be-cauſe of the many great and good actions it produced.   The other great Author needs not be deſcribed, every body knowing too well how low and little he was in many things, even at his height, when Lord Chan-cellor of *England* ; otherwiſe his diſgrace had never been able to deject him ſo much :. The Sun appears as glorious at his ſetting, as riſing ; and I am apt to think whoever behaves himſelf well, and is equal to his advancement, will never appear leſs conſide-rable, or be dejected with his diſgrace. But, to make him ſome amends ; all his works are, for expreſſion as well as thought, the glory of our nation, and of all latter ages.

'T is therefore an amazing thing to reflect on the vaſt difference between the actions and writings of the ſame perſon ! 'Tis enough, almoſt to make a man believe Inſpiration : but to that the Poets only can pretend.   I do not remember that any eminent one of that divine profeſſion, fell thus ſhort in their behaviour of their own former precepts, or acted ſo much contrary to them.   To all this we can only ſay, that of Underſtand-
ings,

ings, as well as Faces, there are no two in
the whole world exactly alike; and therefore in so vast a variety there muft needs be
some very odd and unaccountable. Yet few
fuch wonders as thefe two happen, who were
fo often failing themfelves, yet capabie and
worthy of inftructing all mankind. Such
men put me in mind of one of the beft
Teachers to dance in all *Paris*, who was fo
lame himfelf, that he could hardly go or
ftand.

THESE great Authors had done the world
yet more fervice in their works, if they had
entertain'd us with their own imperfections,
and defcrib'd (as they could have done moft
admirably) that unpliablenefs of their paffions
and humours, under all their learning and
wifdom. But we muft never expect fo much
fincerity in any writer, except the incompa-
rable MONTAGN, who is like to ftand alone
to all pofterity. Yet whenever any great
Wit fhall incline to the fame free way of
writing, I almoft dare affure him of fuccefs;
for befides the agreeablenefs of fuch a book,
fo very fincere a temper of mind needs not
blufh to be expofed as naked as poffible.

MONTAGN, methinks, reprefents ADAM
in his innocence; the very firft of his kind;

R 2 naked,

naked, but not afhamed, becaufe unblemifhed
and unaffected. I know he is accus'd of Vanity, but (I think) without reafon. And
tho' he were guilty, 'tis hard not to forgive
an only fault in him, and a fault which
abounds fo much more in all the great Wits
we read of. Nay, perhaps it is a fault in an
author quite to want it; for why fhould a
man fet up fchool, if he does not own he
knows more than his fcholars? They'll fay,
you muft conceal this good opinion of your
felf; which yet is allowing the thing, tho'
not the fhewing it: and that is fufficient to
excufe MONTAGN, who if he had vanity,
did (fure) of all the world difguife it the
beft; and fo very well, that we fee 'tis a
difpute whether he had it or not? 'Tis indeed the fhewing it felf fo groffly, that is
the foolifh part of vanity; and ruins the reputation it defigns fo much to raife. For
Boafting is not only telling of Lyes, but alfo
many unfeemly Truths; and that man does
certainly worfe who expofes his Miftrefs's
favours, than he who pretends falfely to
have received them; becaufe they are equally
vain, but the firft is alfo ungrateful.

O F

O F

Vulgar Errors.

PROFANENESS in converſation paſ-ſes for ſprightlineſs and wit ; whereas 'tis only a ſign of wanting both Judgment and Manners.

BEING complemental and cringing on all occaſions, paſſes with many for good breeding ; whereas 'tis juſt the contrary. For good breeding is judging well when to be formal, and when to be familiar. Too much of the firſt is as ridiculous on the one hand, as a Quaker's ſcrupling to put off his Hat, on the other ; and in my opinion the more troubleſome extreme of the two.

SILENT ſort of men are eſteem'd generally the more judicious and thinking ; but 'tis commonly only dulneſs and want of thought :

for

for imagination will hardly let the tongue
lie ſtill: Tho' if a quick ſort of man can
overcome his eagerneſs of ſpeaking ſo much,
he will ſhine the more for his not appearing to aim at it.

PHYSICIANS are commonly believ'd to be
of a profeſſion both honeſt and skilful ; yet
their art is little better than that of a Jugler
or Aſtrologer ; which is no art at all, but
couzening the ignorant. Their whole deſign
(generally ſpeaking) is to delay the *Cure*, as
well as the *Death* of their patients: So
that in truth, the laſt of theſe is no leſs an
injury than the other ; for what is Life worth,
under the uneaſineſs of a languiſhing condition? I except particular friendſhips, which
will ſometimes influence them, (and indeed
even ill people :) but I think a *Salary for
life* a better method than *Fees*, and wou'd
more prevail upon theſe gentlemen to do
their beſt; (tho' alas, how little does their
beſt ſignify?) This is only the caſe in general ; for I doubt not but ſome Phyſicians are
abler and honeſter than the reſt ; and I
have my ſelf had the experience of One,
whoſe skill, honeſty, and friendſhip, has re-
covered the moſt valuable part of my family
out of dangers in which we have almoſt
de-

defpaired of fuccefs, and reftored her to perfect health.

SURGEONS are fomething lefs refpected
than phyficians, which is wrong; theirs being a real art, and one of the moft ufeful
ones, if practifed faithfully, (which I doubt
is very feldom.)

APOTHECARIES are under-valued, but
yet, when men of judgment and practice, are
as ufeful as phyficians, who either have not
time, or will not give it, to attend their patients as they fhould do.

DIVINES are generally thought to be,
and often are, Men of the beft Lives; becaufe indeed for fhame they dare hardly be
otherwife: but if their Morals are well obferved, I doubt they will moft of them appear like other men.

GREAT gravity paffes with moft for wifdom, but is often dulnefs, fometimes affectation, at the beft difagreeable.

TELLING ftories well, paffed for the
beft fort of wit in the laft age, and is fometimes approved of even in this; but 'tis more
a talent of diverfion than value.

A man's temper is more judg'd by his
mien and outfide, though very fallacious,
than by his very behaviour it felf.   I have

known

known a man thought haughty, only becaufe he was fhort-fighted, and could not
know people as he met them : but the fame
man, by miftake, would often bow to his
own fervants; who knew his defect, and
therefore had as little reafon to think him
humble, as others had to think him proud.

THE world is always inclined to think
thofe perfons vain (though never fo far from
it) who have either fuch talents, or fuch
good fortune, as would make a great many
others fo. For this reafon, the firft thing
women fay of a new beauty, is, that fhe is
proud and conceited, even before they have
feen her; becaufe they wou'd be fo in her
condition.

WOMEN are thought generally by nature to be much inferior to man in Underftanding; but I believe the difference lies
chiefly in education, by which they give us
very great odds; and yet I know fome that
can hold up the game pretty well againft
us.

WOMEN are believed extremely timorous
too; indeed they are fo of fwords and guns,
becaufe fo little ufed to them; but in other
matters not lefs dangerous, we find them
fufficiently hazardous. Certainly their readi-

I

nefs

neſs in finding excuſes on the ſudden, is no ſmall proof of their reſolution ; with which ſort of confidence nature has armed them for their neceſſary defence on all occaſions, eſpecially againſt thoſe dangers to which ſhe moſt inclines them.

A Wife ſometimes, but a Miſtreſs always, thinks her ſelf undone and forſaken, if ſhe finds a man has but once had an affair with another woman : As if a bit or two of ſecond courſe were a ſign that a man wou'd never love mutton again ; whereas, perhaps it is a reaſon not to be nauſeated even with mutton it ſelf, though it came from *Bagſhot,* or *Banſtead-Downs.*

MEMORY is accounted a talent oppoſite to Wit and Underſtanding, whereas indeed 'tis juſt the contrary. I believe the miſtake ariſes from this : A man of ſenſe will never tell a long ſtory, tho' he ſhould remember it never ſo well ; nor will ſuch a man think many things worth his remembring, which a fool perhaps ſets a value upon.

THEY are thought to have read much, who ſpeak of it often ; which is only a ſign of not digeſting what they read ; juſt as a Man's bringing up his ſupper, gives

a

a proof of his eating, but a very difagreeable one.

WHEN ambitious men are much difap- pointed, fome of the ableft of them have been apt, out of peevifhnefs, to give over the world: But often, a little patience is enough to bring things about again.

SOME people are troubling both them- felves and others with making great feafts, which they think is living nobly, and Princes themfelves are unable to efcape them; whereas a conftant way of living politely, is much more eftimable, as well as pleafant.

SCARCE one fat perfon in twenty, but makes himfelf appear a great deal fatter by fine clothes: and ugly women do the fame by their finery.

'TIS the fafhion to carve at one's own table, a terrible trouble! which divided a- mong the company, would be none at all to any one of them.

MUSICIANS, Painters, and even Poets, are generally thought a little fantaftical; but 'tis the ill ones only, that are fo: the good ones in all ages have been eminently other- wife. As VIRGIL and HORACE, SPENCER, MILTON and WALLER, MALHERBE, COR- NEILLE,

NEILLE, and BOILEAU. For Painters, besides thofe of old, RAPHAEL and LEONARDO,
TITIAN, RUBENS, and VANDIKE, all of
them throughly accomplifh'd, and fit for the
greateft affairs. Mufick has fcarce appear'd
in our climate; but the only perfon remarkable for it in *France* (I mean BAPTIST) was
an agreeable Wit, and all his life manag'd
a great and new diverfion there with credit
and profit. The caufe of this error is, the
multitude of odd fellows inclined to fome
one of thefe three amufements, though not
in the leaft fitted by nature for any of them;
fo that being fo filly as to undertake they
know not what, they muft needs appear
fantaftical, becaufe errant coxcombs; imploying foolifhly their whole time in arts
they are incapable of. That which fhews
fo many more fops in Poetry, than in any
other art or fcience, is very plain; for how
can the ableft Critick in that art convince
the moft foolifh Poet of his failings? even
the moft intimate acquaintance is unwilling
to tell a man that he is an Afs; which is
the very cafe, whenever any body pretends
to this accomplifhment without any genius.
Perhaps he may tell him that he is too
lazy

lazy to be a Lawyer, too nice to be a Phyfician, or too gay to be a Prieft: but to be
told he wants either wit or judgment, goes
very hard with a coxcomb.

A

A
LETTER
TO THE
D---- of Sh----

OU accuse me of fin-
gularity in refigning
the Privy Seal with a
good penfion added to
it, and yet afterwards
ftaying in town at a fea-
fon when every body
elfe leaves it; which
you fay is defpifing at once both Court and
Coun-

Country. You defire me therefore to defend myfelf, if I can, by defcribing very particularly in what manner I fpend fo many hours, that appear long to you who know nothing of the matter, and yet, methinks, are but too fhort for me.

No part of this task which you impofe, is uneafy; except the neceffity of ufing the fingular number fo often. That one Letter [I] is a moft dangerous monofyllable, and gives an air of vanity to the modefteft difcourfe whatfoever. But you will remember I write this only by way of apology; and that, under accufation, it is allowable to plead any thing for defence, though a little tending to one's own commendation.

To begin then without more preamble: I rife, now in fummer, about feven a-clock, from a very large bed-chamber (intirely quiet, high, and free from the early fun) to walk in the garden; or, if rainy, in a *Salon* filled with pictures, fome good, but none difagreeable: there alfo, in a row above them, I have fo many portraits of famous perfons in feveral kinds, as are enough to excite ambition in any man lefs lazy, or lefs at eafe, than myfelf.

INSTEAD of a little dozing closet (according to the unwholesome custom of most people) I chuse this spacious room, for all my small affairs, reading books or writing letters; where I am never in the least tired, by the help of stretching my legs sometimes in so long a room, and of looking into the pleasanteft park in the world just underneath it.

VISITS, after a certain hour, are not to be avoided; some of which I own a little fatiguing (tho' thanks to the town's lazinefs, they come pretty late) if the garden was not fo near, as to give a feasonable refreshment between those ceremonious interruptions. And I am more forry than my coachman himself, if I am forced to go abroad any part of the morning. For though my garden is fuch, as by not pretending to rarities or curiofities, has nothing in it to inveagle one's thoughts; yet by the advantage of fituation and profpect, it is able to fuggeft the nobleft that can be; in prefenting at once to view a vaft Town, a Palace, and a magnificent Cathedral. I confefs the laft with all its fplendour, has lefs fhare in exciting my devotion, than the moft common fhrub in my garden: For though I am apt to
be

be sincerely devout in any sort of religious assemblies, from the very best (that of our own Church) even to those of *Jews, Turks*, and *Indians :* Yet the works of nature appear to me the better sort of sermons; and every flower contains in it the most edifying rhetorick, to fill us with admiration of its omnipotent Creator.

AFTER I have dined (either agreeably with friends, or at worst with better company than your country-neighbours) I drive away to a * Place of air and exercise; which some constitutions are in absolute need of: agitation of the body, and diversion of the mind, being a composition for health above all the skill of HIPPOCRATES.

* *Marybone.*

THE small distance of this place from *London,* is just enough for recovering my weariness, and recruiting my spirits, so as to make me fitter than before I set out, for either business or pleasure. At the mentioning the last of these, methinks I see you smile; but I confess myself so changed [which you maliciously, I know, will call decayed] as to my former enchanting delights, that the company I commonly find at home is agreeable enough to make me conclude the evening on a delightful Terrace, or in a Place free

from

from late vifits, except of familiar acquaintance.

By this account you will fee, that moft of my time is conjugally fpent at home; and confequently you will blame my lazinefs more than ever, for not imploying it in a way, which your partiality is wont to think me capable of. Therefore I am obliged to go on with this trifling defcription, as fome excufe for my idlenefs. But how fuch a defcription itfelf is excufable, is what I fhould be very much in pain about, if I thought any body could fee it befides your felf, who are too good a judge in all things to miftake a friend's compliance in a private letter, for the leaft touch of Vanity.

The Avenues to this houfe are along St. James's Park, through rows of goodly Elms on one hand, and gay flourifhing Limes on the other; that for coaches, this for walking; with the Mall lying between them. This reaches to my iron palifade that incompaffes a fquare court, which has in the midft a great bafon with ftatues and water-works; and from its entrance, rifes all the way imperceptibly, 'till we mount to a Terrace in the front of a large Hall, paved with fquare white ftones mixed with a dark-coloured marble ; the walls of it covered with a fett of pictures done in the fchool of RAPHAEL. Out of this, on the right hand we go into a parlour thirty three foot by thirty nine, with a niche fifteen foot broad for a Bufette, paved with white marble, and placed within an arch, with Pilafters of diverfe colours, the upper part of which as high as the ceiling is painted by RICCI.

FROM hence we pafs through a fuite of large rooms, into a bed-chamber of thirty four foot by twenty feven ; within it a large clofet, that opens into a green-houfe.

ON the left hand of the hall are three ftone arches fupported by *Corinthian* pillars, under one of which we go up eight and forty fteps ten foot broad, each ftep of one entire *Portland*-ftone : Thefe ftairs, by the help of two refting-places, are fo very eafy, there is no need of leaning on the iron-ballufter. The walls are painted with the ftory of DIDO ; whom though the Poet was oblig'd to difpatch away mournfully in order to make room for LAVINIA, the better-natured Painter has brought no farther than to that fatal Cave, where the Lovers appear juft entring, and languifhing with defire.

THE

THE roof of this ftair-cafe, which is fifty five foot from the ground, is of forty foot by thirty fix, filled with the figures of Gods and Goddeffes; in the midft is JUNO, conde-fcending to beg affiftance from VENUS, to bring about a marriage which the fates inten-ded fhould be the ruin of her own darling Queen and People. By which that fublime Poet wifely intimates, that we fhould never be over-eager for any thing, either in our purfuits, or our prayers; left what we en-deavour or ask too violently for our inte-reft, fhould be granted us by Providence on-ly in order to our ruin.

THE bas-reliefs and little fquares above are all epifodical paintings of the fame fto-ry: and the largenefs of the whole has ad-mitted of a fure remedy againft any decay of the colours from falt-petre in the wall, by making another of oak-laths four inches within it, and fo primed over like a pic-ture.

FROM a wide Landing-place on the ftairs-head, a great double-door opens into an a-partment of the fame dimenfions with that below, only three foot higher: Notwith-ftanding which, it would appear too low, if the higher *Salon* had not been divided

S 2   from

from it.   The firſt room of this floor has
within it a cloſet of original pictures, which
yet are not ſo entertaining as the delightful
proſpect from the windows.   Out of the ſecond room a pair of great doors give entrance
into the *Salon*, which is thirty five foot
high, thirty ſix broad, and forty five long.
In the midſt of its roof a round picture of
GENTILESCHI eighteen foot in diameter, re-
preſents the Muſes playing in conſort to A-
POLLO, lying along on a cloud to hear them.
The reſt of the room is adorned with paintings relating to Arts and Sciences; and underneath divers original pictures hang all in
good lights, by the help of an upper row of
windows, which drown the glaring.

MUCH of this ſeems appertaining to pa-
rade, and therefore I am glad to leave it to
deſcribe the reſt, which is all for conveni-
ency.   As firſt, a covered-paſſage from the
kitchen without-doors; and another down
to the cellars and all the offices within.
Near this, a large and lightſome back-ſtairs
leads up to ſuch an entry above, as ſecures
our private bed-chambers both from noiſe
and cold.   Here we have neceſſary dreſſing-
rooms, ſervants rooms, and cloſets, from
which are the pleaſanteſt views of all the
                                        houſe,

houfe, with a little door for communication betwixt this private apartment and the great one.

THESE ftairs, and thofe of the fame kind at the other end of the houfe, carry us up to the higheft ftory, fitted for the women and children, with the floors fo contrived as to prevent all noife over my wife's head, during the myfteries of LUCINA.

IN mentioning the court at firft, I forgot the two wings in it, built on ftone arches, which join the houfe by Corridores fupported on Ionic pillars. In one of thefe wings is a large kitchen thirty foot high, with an open cupolo on the top; near it a larder, brew-houfe, and landry, with rooms over them for fervants: the upper fort of fervants are lodged in the other wing, which has alfo two wardrobes and a ftore-room for fruit: On the top of all, a leaden ciftern holding fifty tuns of water, driven up by an engine from the *Thames,* fupplies all the water-works in the courts and gardens, which lie quite round the houfe; through one of which a grafs walk conducts to the ftables, built round a court, with fix coach-houfes and forty Stalls.

S 3

I'LL

I'LL add but one thing, before I carry you into the garden, and that is about walking too, but 'tis on the top of all the house; which being covered with smooth mill'd Lead, and defended by a parapet of ballusters from all apprehension as well as danger, entertains the eye with a far distant prospect of hills and dales, and a near one of parks and gardens. To these gardens we go down from the house by seven steps, into a gravel-walk that reaches cross the whole garden: with a covered arbour at each end of it. Another of thirty foot broad leads from the front of the house, and lies between two groves of tall Lime-trees planted in several equal ranks upon a carpet of grass: the outsides of these groves are bordered with tubs of Bays and Orange-Trees.

AT the end of this broad walk, you go up to a Terrace four hundred paces long, with a large Semicircle in the middle, from whence is beheld the Queen's two parks, and a great part of *Surrey*; then going down a few steps, you walk on the bank of a canal six hundred yards long, and seventeen broad, with two rows of Limes on each side of it.

ON one side of this Terrace, a Wall covered with Roses and Jassemines is made low,

to

to admit the view of a meadow full of cattle juſt under it, [no diſagreeable object in the midſt of a great City] and at each end a deſcent into parterres, with fountains and water-works.

From the biggeſt of theſe parterres we paſs into a little ſquare garden, that has a fountain in the middle, and two green houſes on the ſides, with a convenient bathing apartment in one of them; and near another part of it lies a flower-garden. Below all this, a kitchen-garden full of the beſt ſorts of fruit, has ſeveral walks in it fit for the coldeſt weather.

Thus I have done with a tedious deſcription : Only one thing I forgot, though of more ſatisfaction to me than all the reſt, which I fancy you gueſs already; and 'tis a little cloſet of Books, at the end of that green-houſe which joins the beſt apartment; which, beſides their being ſo very near, are ranked in ſuch a method, that by its mark a very *Iriſh* footman may fetch any book I want.

Under the windows of this cloſet and green-houſe, is a little wilderneſs full of black-birds and nightingales. The Trees, though planted by my ſelf, require lopping

S 4   already

already, to prevent their hind'ring the view of that fine canal in the *Park*.

AFTER all this, to a friend I'll expose my weakness, as an instance of the mind's unquietness under the most pleasing enjoyments. I am oftner missing a pretty gallery in the old house I pulled down, than pleased with a *Salon* which I built in its stead, tho' a thousand times better in all manner of respects.

AND now [*pour fair bonne bouche* with a grave reflection] it were well 'for us, if this incapacity of being intirely contented was as sure a proof of our being reserved for happiness in another world, as it is of our frailty and imperfection in this. I confess the Divines tell us so; but though I believe a future state more firmly than a great many of them appear to do, by their inordinate desires of the good things in this; yet I own my faith is founded, not on those fallacious arguments of preachers, but on that adorable conjunction of unbounded power and goodness, which certainly must some way recompense hereafter, so many thousands of innocent wretches created to be so miserable here.

A

LETTER to Mr. P----,

On the late Difpute about Homer.

YOU defire my opinion as to the late difpute in *France* concerning Homer: And I think it excufable (at an age alas of not much pleafure) to amufe my felf a little in taking notice of a controverfy, than which nothing is at prefent more remarkable (even in a nation who value themfelves fo much upon the *Belles Lettres*) both on account of the illuftrious fubject of it, and of the two perfons ingaged in the quarrel.

THE one, is extraordinary in all the Lyrick-kind of Poetry, even in the opinion of his very adverfary. The other, a Lady (and

2   of

of more value for being *so*) not only of great
Learning, but with a Genius admirably turn'd
to that fort of it which moſt becomes her
Sex, for ſoftneſs, genteelneſs, and promoting
of vertue : and ſuch as (one would think)
is not ſo liable as other parts of ſcholarſhip,
to rough diſputes, or violent animoſity.

Yet it has ſo happen'd that no writers,
even about Divinity it ſelf, have been more
outrageous or uncharitable than theſe two
polite authors ; by ſuffering their judgments
to be a little warped (if I may uſe that expreſſion) by the heat of their eager inclinations, to attack or defend ſo great an Author under debate : I wiſh, for the ſake of
the publick, which is now ſo well entertain'd
by their quarrel, it may not end at laſt in
their agreeing to blame equally a third man,
who is ſo preſumptuous as to cenſure both,
if they ſhould chance to hear of it.

To begin with matter of faƈt. M. D'Acier
has well judg'd, that the beſt of all Poets
certainly deſerv'd a better tranſlation, at leaſt
into *French* proſe, becauſe to ſee it done
in verſe was deſpair'd of : I believe indeed
from a defeƈt in that language, incapable of
mounting to any degree of excellence ſuit-
able to ſo very great an undertaking.

She

SHE has not only perform'd this task as well as profe can do it, (which is indeed but as the wrong fide of tapeftry is able to reprefent the right) fhe has added to it alfo many learned and ufeful annotations. With all which fhe moft obligingly delighted not only her own fex, but moft of ours, ignorant of the *Greek,* and confequently her adverfary himfelf, who frankly acknowledges that ignorance.

'TIS no wonder therefore if in doing this, fhe is grown fo enamour'd of that unfpeakably-charming Author, as to have a kind of horror at the leaft mention of a man bold enough to blame him.

NOW as to M. DE LA MOTTE, he being already defervedly famous for all forts of Lyrick poetry, was fo far introduc'd by her into thofe beauties of the Epick kind, (though but in that way of tranflation) as not to refift the pleafure and hope of reputation by attempting that in verfe, which had been applauded fo much for the difficulty of doing even in profe; knowing how this, well executed, muft extremely tranfcend the other.

BUT, as great Poets are a little apt to think they have an ancient right of being

excus'd

excus'd for vanity on all occafions; he was not content to out-do M. D'Acier, but endeavour'd to out-do Homer himfelf, and all that ever in any age or nation went before him in the fame enterprize; by leaving out, altering, or adding whatever he thought beft.

Against this prefumptuous attempt, Homer has been in all times fo well defended, as not to need my fmall affiftance; yet I muft needs fay, his excellencies are fuch, that for their fakes, he deferves a much gentler touch for his few feeming errors. Thefe, if M. de la Motte had tranflated as well as the reft, with an apology for having retain'd 'em only out of meer veneration; his judgment in my opinion would have appear'd much greater than by the beft of his alterations, though I admit them to be written very finely.

I join with M. de la Motte in wondering at fome odd things in Homer, but 'tis chiefly becaufe of his fublime ones, I was about to fay his divine ones, which almoft furprize me at finding him any where in the fallible condition of human nature.

And now we are wond'ring, I am in a difficulty to guefs, what can be the reafon of all thefe exceptions againft Homer, from one who has himfelf tranflated him, contrary

trary to the general custom of translators. Is there not a little of that in it? I mean the desire to be singular in getting above the title of a translator, though sufficiently honourable in this case. For such an ambition no body has less occasion, than one who is so fine a poet in other kinds; and who must have too much wit to believe, any alterations of another can intitle him to the denomination of an *Epick Poet* himself: though no man in this age seems more capable of being a good one, if the *French* tongue would bear it. Yet in his translation he has done too well, to leave any doubt (with all his faults) that her's can be ever parallell'd with it.

BESIDES, he could not be ignorant, that finding faults is the most easy and vulgar part of a critick; whereas nothing shews so much skill and taste both, as the being throughly sensible of the sublimest excellencies.

WHAT can we say in excuse of all this, but *Humanum est errare?* Since as good a Poet as I believe the *French* language is capable of, and as sharp a Critick as any nation can produce, has by too much censuring HOMER, subjected a translation to censure, that would have otherwise stood the test of the severest adversary. BUT

BUT since he would needs chuse that wrong way of criticism, I wonder he miss'd a stone so ready to be thrown against HOMER, for his filling the Iliad not only with so much slaughter, (for that is to be excused, since a War is not capable of being described without it) but with so many various particulars of wounds and horror, as shew the writer I am afraid so delighted that way himself, as not the least to doubt his reader being so also. Like SPANIOLETTA, whose dismal pictures are the more disagreeable for being always so very movingly painted. Even HECTOR's last parting from his son and ANDROMACHE, hardly makes us amends for his body's being dragg'd thrice round the town. M. DE LA MOTTE in his strongest objection about that dismal combat, has sufficient cause to blame his inrag'd adversary, who here gives an instance that it is impossible to be violent without committing some mistake ; her passion for HOMER blinding her too much to perceive the very grossest of his failings. By which warning I am become a little more capable of impartiality, though in a dispute about that very poet for whom I have the greatest veneration.

M.

M. D'Acier might have confidered a little, that whatever were the motives of M. DE
LA MOTTE to fo bold a proceeding, it could
not darken that fame which I am fure fhe
thinks fhines fecurely even after the vain attempts of PLATO himfelf againft it : caus'd
only perhaps by a like reafon with that of
Madam D'Acier's anger againft M. DE LA
MOTTE, namely, the finding that in profe
his genius (great as it was) could not be capable of the fublime heights of poetry, which
therefore he banifh'd out of his common-
wealth.

NOR were thefe objections to HOMER
any more leffening of her merit in tranflating
him as well as that way is capable of, *viz.*
fully, plainly, and elegantly, than the moft
admirable verfes can be any difparagement
to as excellent profe.

THE beft excufe for all this violence is,
its being in a caufe which gives a kind of
reputation even to fuffering, by never fo ill
a management of it.

THE worft of defending even HOMER in
fuch a paffionate manner, is its being more
a proof of her weaknefs, than of his being
liable to none. For what is it can excufe
HOMER any more than HECTOR, for flying

3   at

at the firſt ſight of ACHILLES? whoſe terrible aſpect ſure needed not ſuch an inexcuſe-
able fright to ſet it off; and methinks all
that account of MINERVA's reſtoring his dart
to ACHILLES, comes a little too late, for
excuſing HECTOR's ſo terrible apprehenſion
at the very firſt.

F I N I S.

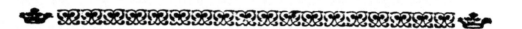

THE

CASTRATIONS.

[Price One Shilling and Six-pence.]

Some Account

OF THE

REVOLUTION.

I N the Year 1688, there was a wonderful Confternation among fome People, and an eager Expectation in All, what would be the Event of an Army's landing in *England*, under the Command of a Prince fo nearly related, and nearer ally'd to the King. The pretended Caufe of his coming was for Redrefs of Grievances; the real one needs not be mentioned, and will be eafily imagined.

THE Nation had been long uneafy, even in fome former Reigns, with Fears of Pope-

a 2

ry

ry and arbitrary Power; and of late many of the very Court and Council appear'd unfatisfied on that Account. Some were vex'd alfo for two other Reafons; the great Diminution of their Salaries, by the ill-timed Retrenchments of the Treafury, and their finding all the Power and Favour engrofs'd by a few, and thofe alfo the foolifheft of the *Roman* Party.

THIS general Diflike of the King's Management, had, like an Infection, reach'd fome of his Minifters themfelves, as the Earls of *Mulgrave* and *Middleton*, never the leaft tainted with being either falfe or factious; yet the firft of them, not only in Execution of his Office, affifted openly all the Proteftant Clergy, but abfented himfelf from all the Councils; and both of them, in their own Juftification, took all Occafions of deriding the ill Advices of the Papifts.

BUT a more dangerous Symptom of the future Change, was a Defertion among the Officers of his Majefty's Army, and, at laft, of the Lord *Churchill* himfelf, tho' a kind of Favourite.

YET all this was nothing, in comparifon of the Princefs's withdrawing her felf from Court by Night, without any Servants, except the Lady *Churchill*, and Mrs. *Berkeley*, con-

conducted by the Bishop of *London*, whose late Disgrace at Court had help'd him to a reverential sort of Popularity, which he, of all the Bishops, would least have found otherwise.

AND because this extraordinary Desertion of one Daughter, as well as the other's sitting on a Father's Throne afterwards, must needs seem wonderful in two such Princesses, both of strict Devotion, and many great Virtues, Posterity perhaps will be glad to have some farther Account of such unprecedented Proceedings in Persons of so unblameable and illustrious a Character.

'TIS very remarkable, that this Prince was so thoroughly unfortunate, as to be undone by his own Children, and the more, by their being bred up most carefully and religiously, and their being endowed with all virtuous Inclinations. These being first deceiv'd, by the indefatigable Industry of some People, drew in a great Part of the Nation to be deceived also, by the Goodness of their Dispositions, and the Nearness of their Relation to the Person accused. For who could suspect such Daughters of wronging their Father? It was infused into them severally by the properest Instruments that could be found, that their Father was

not

not only refolved to perfecute the Proteftant Religion, but to ftick at nothing in order to it; and therefore, at once to prevent his eldeft Daughter's fucceeding him, and to fecure the Throne after him to one of his own Religion, he had contrived a fuppofititious Son, who was to fucceed, and to fettle that which his fuppofed Father might not live long enough to fix fufficiently. And tho' the Juftice of his Mind, and the Tendernefs of his Nature, were enough to difperfe all fuch Apprehenfions; yet the Zeal of Popifh Religion was brought in to overbalance all other Confiderations. All this was joined with the Prince of *Orange's* conjugal Impofitions on the moft complying Wife in the World, who was at laft drawn into the difmal Neceffity of giving up either her Husband, or a Father, refolved and ready (as fhe thought) to difinherit her. So that two worthy religious Ladies, even becaufe they were fo, confented to dethrone a moft indulgent Father, and to fucceed him boldly, in their feveral Turns, before an innocent Brother then a Child.

Tantum Religio, &c.

'Tis no wonder, after this, if the King began to miftruft every body; which made
him

him on a fudden leave his Army at *Salif-bury*, in order to confider his Condition more fecurely at *London*. And here I muft obferve his ill Fortune, in depending on his Army at firft too much, and now at laft too little. For 'tis very probable, that his Soldiers, if once blooded, would have gone on with him, and have beaten the Prince of *Orange*, juft as he done before the Duke of *Monmouth*; the Nature of *Englifhmen* being like that of our Game-cocks, which an *Irifh* Footman once thought he might truft fafely together, becaufe they were match'd on one Side, but quickly found them picking out one another's Eyes. The Truth is, our Countrymen love no Caufe, nor Man, fo well as Fighting, even fometimes without any Caufe at all.

I N quitting his Army thus fuddenly, the King was thought too fufpicious and precipitate: But (as unlucky Betters will lofe on both Sides) he had juft before err'd as much by his Dilatorinefs, as he did now by his Hafte; for when the Lord *Churchill* deferted him at *Salisbury*, he fent Orders immediately to feize all his Papers at *Whitehall*, before he had fecur'd either his Lady or the Princefs, which was only frightening the one, and difobliging the other.

W H E N

WHEN the King was return'd from *Salisbury*, his Council was reduced within a very narrow Compass; and, since he ever before thought no body entirely in his Interest, except they were of his Religion also; 'tis no wonder, if, at this suspicious Time, he consulted with a few Papists only; who (being the very Persons most obnoxious to a Parliament, whenever summon'd, and to the Rabble, if Things ran to Confusion) unanimously advis'd him to fly; but more for their own sakes than his, because they might hope to have an Interest with him, remaining in *France*, whither they were now forc'd to escape themselves. From hence alone came that fatal Resolution of his retiring; which was perhaps the Loss of his Crown, but certainly some Diminution to his former Reputation.

THE King, however, resolv'd to try one Remedy first, or, at least, by that to disguise his intended Flight the better; and therefore summon'd all the Peers in Town to a kind of General Council in *Whitehall*; at which some of the Bishops, as well as Temporal Lords, open'd their Grievances so boldly, that he condescended to send two of them (*viz.* the Marquess of *Halifax*, and the Earl of *Nottingham*) as his Commissioners

ners to the Prince of *Orange*; joining the Lord *Godolphin* with them, who was the only Man that had the Cunning, or elfe the good Fortune, to be at once in fome Favour with both the King and Prince of *Orange*.

In the mean time he fent away the Queen, in all Hafte and Privacy, under the Conduct of Monfieur *Lauzun*, an old difgrac'd Favourite of the *French* King; which indeed was enough to difcover his own Intention of going to *France* foon after. But it was thought worth incurring that Sufpicion, to fecure the Prince of *Wales*, whom fhe carry'd along with her to *Calâis*. After which, the King, (who before judged himfelf under a Neceffity of leaving the Kingdom) began now to grow under an Impatience alfo; and perhaps indulged his uneafy Thoughts, with reflecting, that he now abandon'd three Kingdoms, not fo much to fave himfelf, as to follow a Wife and only Son.

Just as he was ftepping into Bed, the Night before his going away, the Earl of *Mulgrave* happened to come into the Bed-chamber, which being at fo late an Hour, might poffibly give the King fome Apprehenfion of that Lord's fufpecting his Defign, with which he was refolved not to truft

him.

him, nor any other Proteſtant whatſoever. He therefore ſtopp'd ſhort, and turn'd about to whiſper him in the Ear, that his Commiſſioners had newly ſent him a very hopeful Account of ſome good Accommodation with the Prince of *Orange:* To which that Lord only reply'd with a Queſtion, asking him, if the Prince's Army halted, or approach'd nearer to *London?* The King own'd they ſtill march'd on ; at which the other ſhook his Head, and ſaid no more, only made him a low Bow, with a dejected Countenance, humbly to make him underſtand, that he gave no Credit to what the King's hard Circumſtances at that time obliged him to diſſemble.

Thus reſerved was the King to every Body about his withdrawing himſelf ; as indeed Men are generally moſt cloſe in Secrets againſt their own Intereſt. The myſterious Carriage of this abſconding coſt the Lord Chancellor *Jefferies* his Life (a thing indeed of little Value to any Body beſides himſelf) who died afterwards in Priſon, for want of having the ſame Warning given him to eſcape, which had been given to the Earl of *Melford* and Father *Peters.* This Proceeding of his was imputed to neither ill Nature nor Careleſsneſs, two

Faults

Faults his Majesty was not guilty of; but rather to his Generosity; which made him compassionate his very Enemies so much, as never to forgive that Lord's Cruelty in executing such Multitudes of them in the West, against his express Orders.

THE Nuntio also escaped very narrowly; for, after having stolen away to *Gravesend*, behind the Coach of an Envoy of *Savoy*, he was there perceived by the Earl of *Winchelsea*, who, tho' Lord Lieutenant of the County, had been unable to preserve him from the Rabble; and therefore sent immediate Notice of it to the *Spanish* Ambassador; who as speedily caus'd the Prince of *Orange* to be waked at *Windsor*, and to sign a particular sort of Passport for the Train of that *Savoy* Minister. By this they prevented an Accident that would have made an ill Impression at this time upon all the Prince's Confederates of the *Roman* Catholick Religion.

BUT, to return to the King. At Three o' Clock in the Morning, he withdrew himself by a back Way out of the Bed-chamber; commanding the Duke of *Northumberland* (whom he left there on a Pallet Bed, according to the Custom of his Place

of

of Gentleman of the Bed-chamber in waiting) not to open the Door, before his usual Hour of rising, at which time, several Persons of Quality, according to Custom, in great Numbers, being come to attend him at his Levee, divulged the News immediately of his being gone away.

THE King intending to pass thro' *Kent* to the Sea-side, took with him Sir *Edward Hales*, a Gentleman of a great Estate there, and a new Convert, which had drawn on him the Hatred of all that Country, to so great a Degree, as to make him a Hindrance, instead of a Help to their Escape. This the King himself told us at his Return from *Feversham*, admiring at Sir *Edward*'s having so little Credit in his own County : Which was so right an Image, in little, of his own unfortunate Condition, that it had been enough to make him more cautious, if he could have perceived it sooner.

THE King's sudden absenting himself, as it was very extraordinary, so it produced as extraordinary Effects every where.

IN the Prince of *Orange*'s Army, the Nation was look'd on as their own ; at least, all the good Employments in it. In *London*, all the Lords there, both Spiritual and

and Temporal, met the Mayor and Aldermen at *Guildhall*, who, with the reft of
the Citizens, were under fuch a Confternation, that they all entirely fubmitted to
the Conduct of thofe few Peers, who were
almoft in as much Apprehenfion themfelves:
For, indeed, the Rabble were the Mafters,
if the Beafts had known their own Strength;
at leaft, till the Prince's Army arriv'd at
London, which then took their Turn in being fo, tho' but one Degree better. One
of the Lords, in the Name of all the reft,
affured the City Magiftrates of their Affection and Care for the publick Safety;
after which, they retired into a Room appointed for them, and chufing Mr. *Gwin*
and Mr. *Cooling* to act the Part of Secre-
taries, who had been fo before to the Earls
of *Rochefter* and *Mulgrave*, two Lords then
prefent; they fent Letters immediately to
the Fleet, the abandon'd Army of King
James, and to all the confiderable Garrifons
in *England*, which kept them all in Order
and Subjection, not only to the prefent
Authority, but to that which fhould be
fettled afterwards.

THE Citizens were extreamly appre-
henfive of the *Tower*, imagining all their
Houfes would tumble down at the firft
Gun

Gun that ſhould be ſhot from thence; on which the Lords took Occaſion of the Lieutenant's Abſence, at ſuch a time, to put that Command into the Hands of the Lord *Lucas,* who had the good Fortune to be quarter'd there with his Company of Foot. But the moſt important Act of this Aſſembly, was their ſending one Peer of each Rank with a Letter to the Prince of *Orange,* ſubſcribed by them all, in which they took Notice of the King's Abſence, and the Neceſſity of his making all Expedition to *London,* in order to the publick Quiet. This Addreſs was ſign'd by the * Archbiſhop of *Canterbury* in the firſt Place, whom I particularly mention, becauſe, after this ſingle Act of Compliance, he never would appear in publick Affairs, or pay the leaſt ſort of Reſpect to the Prince of *Orange,* even after he was elected King of *England;* and yet, on the other Side, had been as moroſe to King *James* before, in never acknowledging his Son, or ſhewing him the leaſt Civility.

WHILE the Lords thus acted in the City, they often ſent for the Lord Mayor, who received all their Orders as ſub-

* *Sancroft.*

miſſively;

missively, as if they had been the most legal Commands; and when this Assembly rose, the People were so sensible of their Dignity, or rather of their Care to prevent all Disorders, that several of them, even the two Lords before mentioned, tho' Ministers of the unfortunate King, had their Coaches attended with Crowds and Applauses as far as the City-gates. Which I purposely take Notice of, because it is a most remarkable Instance of the Advantage and Power which Men of Rank have above others, whenever they shew themselve industrious and zealous for the publick Good.

FROM this Time forwards, 'till the King's Return out of *Kent*, these Lords met every Day in the Council-chamber at *Whitehall*; and by that prevented the Unruliness of the Rabble, who, the first Hour after the King's absconding, pull'd down the Houses of the *Florentine* Envoy, and the *Spanish* Ambassador; the last of whom had full Amends made him, notwithstanding so high an Insolence: For the Earl of *Mulgrave* (tho' his Master was gone, and his Staff laid aside) yet thought the Honour of the Nation so much concerned, that he presum'd to take upon himself to
order

order an Apartment in *Whitehall* immediately, and a great Table to be kept for him twice a Day, with Yoemen of the Guard to attend in his outward Room (which they never do but on the King only) for which Strain of Authority he had the Fortune to thanked both by King *James* and the Prince of *Orange*. This was the highest Respect that could possibly be paid to the King of *Spain* his Master; and yet for himself, a better Reparation was made afterwards by King *William*, who gave him 17000 *l.* in lieu of his pretended Losses; but it rather was for his good Service in persuading all the House of *Austria* to acknowledge him King, to which they were a great while extreamly averse, notwithstanding their Union with him against *France* and King *James*.

THE Bishop of *Canterbury* refusing to come any more among those Lords who met at *Whitehall*, and the Archbishop of *York* being unaccustomed to the Business of such an Assembly, a Lord before-named, one Day propos'd the Marquess of *Halifax* as a fit Person to preside in it, which being agreed to, happened to be the Cause of all his Favour with the Prince of *Orange*; who, finding him in that Manner at the
Head

Head of fuch a Council, and indeed ready
to ferve any Turn, thought he might be
ufeful in this Conjuncture; tho' before,
he had always forbidden his Agents ever
to truft him with their Defign of coming
into *England.* He was accordingly ftill
forced to undergo an eafy fort of Tryal,
before that Party would entirely confide in
him; which was after this manner. When
the King unexpectedly return'd from *Fever-*
fham, they refolved in the Prince's Council,
that fome Perfons fhould be fent to *White-*
hall, with an imperious fort of Meffage in
the Dead of Night, to make him underftand, the Prince look'd on him as his Prifoner, and accordingly expected he would
immediately remove to *Ham,* under a
Guard of *Dutchmen.* The Earl of *Shrewf-*
bury, and the Lord *Delamere* willingly undertook this extraordinary Embaffy; but
the Prince added the Marquefs of *Halifax*
to be at the Head of it; and could not help
fmiling (as he own'd afterwards) to fee him,
who came a Commiffioner to him from the
other Side, accept to act fo low a Part fo
very willingly. All this was after the King's
being difcover'd in *Kent,* before which time
the Peers fat daily in the Council-chamber
at *Whitehall,* where the Lord *Mulgrave*

one Morning happen'd to be advertised privately, that the King had been seiz'd by the angry Rabble of *Feversham*, and had sent a poor Countryman with the News, in order to procure his Rescue: Which was like to come too late, since the Messenger had waited long at the Council-door, without any body's being willing to take Notice of him. This sad Account mov'd him with great Compassion, at such an extraordinary Instance of worldly Uncertainty; and no Cautions of offending the prevailing Party, were able to restrain him from shewing a little Indignation at so mean a Proceeding in the Council. Upon which, their new President adjourn'd it hastily, in order to prevent him; but that Lord earnestly conjur'd them all to sit down again presently, that he might acquaint them with a Matter which admitted of no Delay, and was of the highest Importance imaginable. Accordingly, the Lords, who knew nothing of the Business, could not but hearken to it; and those few that guess'd it, and saw the Consequence, yet wanted Time for concerting enough together about so nice, and so very important a Matter, as saving or losing a King's Life. The Lords therefore sat down again, and he then re-

presented

prefented to them what a Barbarity it would be, for fuch an Affembly to connive at the Rabble's tearing in Pieces even any private Gentleman, much more, a Great Prince, who, with all his Popery, was ftill their Sovereign. So that meer Shame obliged them to fufpend their Politicks a-while, and to call in the Meffenger, who told them with Tears, how the King had with much Difficulty engag'd him to deliver a Letter from him to any Perfons whom he could find willing to fave him from fo imminent Danger. The Letter had no Superfcription, and was to this Effect: To acquaint the Reader of it, that he had been difcover'd in his Retreat by fome Fifhermen of *Kent*, and fecur'd at firft there by the Gentry, who were yet afterwards forc'd to refign him into the Hands of an infolent Rabble.

ON fo preffing an Occafion, and now fo very publickly made known, the Council was furpriz'd, and under fome Difficulty: For, as there was Danger of difpleafing, by doing their Duty, fo there was no lefs, by omitting it; fince the Law makes it highly criminal to be only paffive in fuch an Extremity: Befides, that moft of them, unacquainted as yet with the Prince of

Orange,

Orange, imagin'd him prudent, and confequently capable of punifhing fo bafe a Defertion, either out of Generofity or Policy. Thefe found afterwards their Caution needlefs; but at prefent it influenc'd the Council enough to make them fend Two Hundred of the Life-guard, under the Command of their Captain, the Earl of *Feverfham*, firft to fecure the King from all Danger of the common People, and afterward to attend him toward the Sea-fide, if he continued his Refolution of retiring ; which they thought it more decent to connive at, than to detain him here by Force.

B u t it feems he was prevail'd on to lay afide, or rather defer his Journey to *France*, till a farther Opportunity ; and it is not unlikely, that trufting no body at that time, he might only pretend to be convinc'd of his Error in going away, in order to get a better Opportunity for it at *London*, than he could hope for in that Country, where he was fo narrowly watch'd, under the Pretence of being only guarded. But, whatever his Defign was, the Shouts of Joy, and Shew of Welcome which attended his Coach through *London*, both ftartled his Enemies, and inclined him a little to flight his Friends; openly blaming in Council all thofe

thofe Peers, who, in his Abfence, and out
of meer Neceffity, had taken on themfelves
a Power that was fo very ufeful to the publick Quiet. Which fhews how jealous of
their Authority Princes are apt to be, tho'
nothing can more endanger them, than fuch
an overftraining it.

THE King's Return altered all the Mea-
fures taken in the Prince of *Orange*'s Camp,
which was by this time become a Court,
and all Places fuppofed to be at their Difpofal. The Prince, who needed Counfel
fometimes, had now more Occafion than
ever, to affemble all thofe about him, who
were either of Quality or Confideration
enough for it. Some, who yet have been
fince the greateft *Jacobites* and *Nonjurors*,
propos'd the fending King *James* to the
Tower, and hinted at fomething farther.
But even the worft-humour'd Princes are
lefs fevere than Counfellors on fuch Occafions, efpecially to Perfons of their own
Rank, with whom they cannot avoid having a kind of Fellow-feeling. Whether (as
fome partial to him have imagined) it proceeded either from Generofity, or fome
Promife made to his Wife at Parting; or
whether he was made believe, that neither
the King's Death nor Imprifonment would
help

help him to the Crown so soon, as his Escaping into *France*, a Country so hated by the *English*; or whether he might apprehend his Wife's Title would be found better than his own, in Case of her Father's being dead: On which soever of these Grounds it was, the Prince of *Orange* at last resolved to connive at the King's going into *France*, and to preserve him from Violence in order to it.

ACCORDING to the Design of sending him away by the Despair of any Accommodation, the Earl of *Feversham* (whom the King sent to the Prince with a Compliment) was, instead of a civil Reception, clapt into Prison immediately; and Mr. *Zuylestein* was sent in all Haste to *Kent*, to forbid the King's approaching to *London*.

BUT the King was arrived there before, in the midst of many joyful Acclamations, which obliged the Prince to dally no longer, and to send those three Lords beforementioned, in such a Manner as might seem almost to pronounce his Doom. They affectedly came about Midnight, and rather exacted, than desired Admittance to his Bed-side at that unseasonable Hour; where the Marquess of *Halifax* inform'd him from the Prince, that it was dangerous to his

Maje:

Majefty, as well as to the publick Peace, to remain in *London* ; and fo defired his immediate going to *Ham*, a Houfe near it, belonging to the Duchefs of *Lauderdale*.

THE King underftood the Meffage, as well as his Danger in being refractory, therefore only defired *Ham* might be changed for *Rochefter*, a Town not far from the Sea Coaft of *France* ; to which the Lords foon brought him the Prince's Confent ; and fo he was conveyed thither by Water, under a Guard of * Fifty *Dutchmen*, whofe Officer had private Orders to let him efcape afterwards to *France*.

I MUST not omit two things, which fhew'd his Temper under fuch an unexpected Change. When the ftout Earl of *Craven* refolved to be rather cut in Pieces, than to refign his Poft at *Whitehall* to the Prince's Guards, the King prevented that unneceffary Bloodfhed with a great deal of Care and Kindnefs: And amidft all that juft Apprehenfion of Violence to his Perfon, at the fudden Entry into his Chamber of thofe three Lords, he at leaft difguis'd it fo well, as to difcourfe about the ferving of the Tide, and other things relating to

---

* There was Fifty Horfe and an Hundred Foot of the Prince's Guards.

his

his Removal, as coolly, and unconcernedly, as if it had been only a common Journey.

THE same Night that the King was sent thus to *Rochester*, the Prince of *Orange* came to *London*; where the People were so frighted with a Report artificially spread about some *Irish* Papists intending a Massacre, and with the usual Insolence of a Rabble, that he was received with a seeming Satisfaction.

THE next Day he summoned all the Lords in Town to St. *James*'s where he kept his Court, and after he had in a few Words opened the pretended Cause of his coming, he desired them to consider of the fittest Means to accomplish the good Ends and Promises in his Declaration; which, as it was the first time, so it was also the last, that ever he seem'd to remember those Promises, during all his Reign.

THE Lords accordingly met him next Day at *Westminster*, where they only chose the Marquess of *Halifax* for their Speaker, and made an Order against any Papists appearing about the House of Parliament. But, on *Monday* following, Notice was brought to the Lords, of the King's being escaped from *Rochester*, according to the before-mentioned tacit Agreement about that

that Matter between him and the Prince; who let him go, only becaufe he thought his efcaping into *France* would be the fureft Means of helping him to poffefs his Place here. Of this the King himfelf was fenfible, and therefore, as foon as ever his Life was fecure, he contrived to leave a Letter behind him directed to the Earl of *Middleton*, in which he appeal'd both to God and Man againft his Flight, forc'd upon him by fo near a Relation. His Courtiers moved to have this Letter read, but it was carried by Vote in the Negative; which was the firft Proof of the Lords Intention of excluding their King, though many Divifions arofe among them afterwards about the Way of doing it.

THEY all agreed alfo now in two things, the moft important that could be. The firft was, that a Convention fhould be fummoned by circular Letters in the Prince of *Orange*'s Name, to all thofe Places which have a Right of chufing Members of Parliament: And fecondly, that the Prince fhould be defired to manage all publick Affairs, as well as all publick Monies, in the mean time.

SOME who had Eftates in *Ireland*, defired the Care and Prefervation of that im-

portant

portant Kingdom might be particularly inserted into that Address; which was something oddly opposed by the New-Court Party (for their sure Expectation of a new King warrants me now to call them so) but yet the Reason and meer Necessity of the thing proposed, forced them to comply with it at last.

It may be wondered at, and scarce believed hereafter, that a full House of Noblemen, wherein were so many of the old Court and Council, should agree so readily to lay aside their King, and not so much as read the Letter that he left behind him, which might almost be reckoned the last Words of a dying Sovereign: But that was the Cause of it, being thought dangerous, and too moving to be read. It must also be consider'd, that of late, both the King's Actions, and the Prince of *Orange*'s (even as if they had agreed it between them) tended to the possessing every Body with a strong Opinion, of the Protestant Religion being endanger'd by the one, and protected by the other. This made almost all the King's Ministers, as well as his Courtiers, expect more Favour even under this new Prince, than they were like to find among a few Bigots of a Religion that endures

dures no other. Therefore, fince Zeal in fome, and Intereſt in all, co-operated againſt the King, we need look for no farther Reaſons of ſo ſudden a Change.

BESIDES all this, we may reaſonably conclude, that ſome few Perſons meaning the Prince no good, might think it imprudent to ſtem a Tide, to no other Purpoſe, except their own Ruin: And therefore rather reſerved that Intereſt (which, by their Compliance, they obtained both with the Prince and People) to ſecure the publick Good as much as poſſible, in a Seaſon when almoſt every Body ſeem'd to abandon it. For ſome of the old *Whiggs*, who had ſo long deſpair'd of Court Favour, were now ſo tranſported with it, not only out of their old Principles, but even out of their very Senſes alſo, that ſuch a good Opportunity was loſt, of re-ſettling our old Conſtitution, as perhaps *England* is never like to have again. Which I do not obſerve with any Regard to either of the Kings in Competition; but I only mean, that (whichſoever Prince that Conſtitution ſhould ſet up) our Liberties might have been ſecured, and the Government fixed, on the beſt and ſteadieſt Foundations, an united Intereſt of King and People.

THIS

THIS Addreſs of the Lords, inveſting the Prince with almoſt Regal Power, tho' ſufficiently welcome, was yet a little perplexing: For as he could not but think it dangerous to dally with ſuch an Offer; ſo, on the other Hand, it was not very ſafe to accept it, without the Approbation of the Commons alſo.

THE Difficulty lay in this; that he could have that Approbation neither formally, nor plainly, without firſt aſſembling a Parliament; which yet itſelf alone was ſo great an Act of Sovereignty, that, to call it by the Lords Advice only, was, in a manner, accepting the Regal Power from them.

HE was better adviſed in this, than in moſt other things; for a good Expedient was reſolved on. He reply'd, that he would conſider of their Addreſs, and, in the mean time, aſſembled at St. *James*'s all thoſe in Town, who had been Members of King *Charles*'s two laſt Parliaments, together with the Lord Mayor, Court of Aldermen, and Fifty Repreſentatives of the Common Council, whom he deſired to conſider the extraordinary Neceſſity of coming preſently to ſome good Reſolution.

ACCORDINGLY, they all went to *Weſtminſter* next Day, where, in the uſual
House

House of Commons (chusing Mr. *Powell* for their Speaker) they imitated the Lords, in making exactly the same Address. And indeed both Houses might well concur in all, since influenc'd, I might have said enforc'd, by the same Causes; which last Expression I make use of, both on account of the Prince's Army here, commanded by a famous General, the *Mareschal de Schomberg*, and also of a Murmur which went about, that the City Apprentices were coming down to *Westminster* in a violent Rage against all who voted against the Prince of *Orange*'s Interest. And 'tis certain, that some hot-headed Persons were hardly restrained by the Prince of *Orange* himself, who lik'd their Zeal, but found no need of using such a sort of Means, as might justly invalidate all that should be then done in his Favour.

As soon as they had thus publickly address'd to the Prince, and every Man had privately adjusted his own Conditions with him, both Houses dissolved themselves, in order to go into their several Countries to influence the approaching Election of that Convention which was to settle all things.

'Tis easily imagin'd, that all possible Industry was used, for chusing only Persons
ill-

ill-affected] to the unhappy King, which (for that only Reason, because he was so) were not very difficult to find. But it happened also, that the *Church-party* was almost as much oppos'd as the *Jacobites,* because inclin'd to set up the Princess of *Orange,* above even the Prince her Husband; notwithstanding that he was here, arm'd, and she was absent. For this Reason she was kept in *Holland,* 'till he had master'd that Difficulty, which vex'd him more than any other.

THERE was Opposition also from her Sister the Princess of *Denmark,* who thought it hard to lose her Rank of Succession, by yielding the Crown to him who was but the second Branch, and of whom she had deserved so well: And now both these Sisters were assisted in their several Pretensions by the *Church-party,* for one Reason only, *viz.* because they were bred up extreamly devoted to it.

ONE of the Prince's Arguments (tho' he gave some more solid ones, that seldom fail to persuade) was indeed a little extraordinary; for he very gravely endeavour'd to make his Friends believe, that he would leave them all in the Lurch, by returning with his Army into *Holland,* rather than yield

yield the Title to his own Wife: And a-while he oppofed (tho' to no Purpofe) even her being joined with himfelf in the Sovereignty. Which fhews the extream Reftlefsnefs of Ambition, even in its higheft Scenes of Succefs. For, tho' an almoft extravagant Expedition had thus luckily fucceeded, even beyond his utmoft Hopes; yet, upon this Jealoufy, he grew more uneafy, than perhaps ever in his Life before.

On this Account he grew jealous of his moft intimate Confidents among the *Englifh*, becaufe they had fo much Regard to his Wife, with whom he liv'd always coldly, and a little imperioufly (imitating in that *Henry* VIII.) tho' her conftant and moft remarkable Compliance with him, even againft her own Father and Principles alfo, had been a mighty Help to all his Defigns.

At this Time, among other Confultations held in feveral Places about thefe Matters, there was one appointed at Mr. *William Herbert*'s Lodgings in St. *James*'s, who was then fick of the Gout, and fo concern'd at the Great Favourite's urging it was beft to make the Princefs no Sovereign, and only a Queen Confort; that, rifing out of Bed with Earneftnefs, he protefted againft
ever

ever drawing a Sword on the Prince's Side, if he could have imagin'd him capable of such Usage to his Wife. This so alarm'd and convinc'd Monf. *Bentinck*, of the Impossibility of obtaining a Point, which even so interested a Courtier as *Herbert* refus'd to comply in, that in half an Hour's time he brought them Affurance from the Prince of his not insisting on it, and of his being content with conjunctive Sovereignty, on Condition he might have the sole Adminition; which last they confented to, becaufe herself so defired it.

THE Pretensions of the Princefs of *Denmark* were more easily accommodated: For, since the Lord *Churchill* (who govern'd that Family) was like to be highly favoured in this new Reign, they little thought of hers. And therefore, with a good Bribe to her Favourite, the Prince had no more to do, but to promise the Princefs a great Penfion by a Settlement in Parliament; which being in present, and enough to keep her Court in Splendor, was then thought equivalent to three Kingdoms in Reverfion.

THUS were all things difpos'd of for the Convention in the Cabals on the Prince of *Orange*'s Side; and it met on the 22d of *January*. The Prince fent to both Houfes

Houſes a Letter, urging them to all imaginable Expedition, under the Pretence of
common Dangers. But as ſoon as the Lords
had choſen the Marqueſs of *Halifax* again
for their Speaker, a Letter was ſtraight
brought in, directed to the Speaker of that
Houſe: And it appearing by the Bearer of
it, Mr. *Gray*, that it was given him by the
Earl of *Melford* at St. *Germaine*'s in *France*,
where our King then liv'd, the Lords with
a kind of Clamour forbad it to be read.
By which it appear'd plainly, what was
like to follow againſt that unhappy Prince;
tho' they ſtill divided about the Manner of
excluding him.

Now this is the Place, where I would
ſpare no Care I am capable of, to explain
all thoſe ſecret Turns in that famous Aſſembly, which at laſt made a new Settlement
of the Crown of *England* (I wiſh I could
ſay, of it's Prerogative alſo, by the juſt
bounding of which all our Liberties ſubſiſt)
but alas! that was the leaſt Thought of
thoſe who dethron'd a King, and impo-
veriſh'd a Nation, under that Pretence
only.

THE Houſe of Commons was the moſt
unanimous in the new Courtſhip; and
therefore it was thought wiſeſt to begin
this

this great Bufinefs there ; from whence they
fent up to the Lords this following Vote:
*That the King, by having witdrawn himfelf
out of the Kingdom, had abdicated the Government, and fo the Throne was become vacant.*

The Houfe of Lords was extreamly full,
fcarce one of them was abfent, except the
Papifts ; and it was divided into three Parties : That of the *High-Church* inclin'd to
the Princeffes ; thofe whom we now call
Whiggs, affured of good Imployments under
the Prince ; and a Third, very much the
fmalleft, inclin'd to the unfortunate King,
fome out of Confcience, but more out of
Defpair of Favour from the Prince.

Left Unfinifh'd.

A FEAST

A
FEAST
OF THE
GODS.

A S SENSIBLE Men, of all Degrees, shew their Prudence, not only in rightly managing their Affairs, but also in seeking out for themselves some Sort of Pleasures and Diversions; finding by Experience, that our Minds, no less than our Bodies, require a Relaxation, in order to be the more active and vigorous afterwards; so, even the Gods themselves, tho' far above the Frailties of poor Mortals, yet are reported by *Homer*, and all the Poets of old, sometimes to suspend their graver Considerations, and, in plain *English*, take a Cup of *Nectar* together.

ONE of these merry Meetings was appointed t'other Day by *Jupiter*, who sent *Mercury* (from whom I received the following Account) to invite the whole Set of

Gods

Gods and Goddesses to that illustrious Assembly.

AFTER they had fill'd their Bellies with *Ambrosia*, they began to talk a little freely of all their several sorts of Worlds, some of which we ignorant Men call Planets, and fancy them made only for us to gaze on.

WHEN they had rambled over many of the more considerable Globes, they fell upon this of ours at last ; but finding in it more Occasion for their Anger than their Mirth, were e'en just going to annihilate it (which to the Gods is no more than breaking a Glass among Good-fellows, when they find it dirty) if *Momus* had not burst out into a sudden Fit of Laughter at a certain Creature in it call'd Man ; who (he undertook) should be a Subject able to furnish Sport enough for the whole Feast, if they would but, for once, connive at his Faults, and only expose his Follies.

VENUS a little blush'd at this, for the sake (as it was guess'd) of *Adonis, Anchises*, and half a Hundred more Gallants of hers: Then pertly reprehended *Momus*, for making so bold with a Creature that was ever accounted the very Image of the Gods ; and for the sake of some of which, only to please his Fancy, Almighty *Jupiter* had
vouch-

vouchfaf'd to transform himfelf into a mortal Shape. But *Vulcan* bid her be filent for Shame, telling them he faw no fuch great Difference between Creatures of two Legs, and thofe of four, except in Vanity, in which the firft Sort did fo much abound, as prefumptuoufly to arrogate the Preheminence above all their Brethren, nay, profanely pretend to refemble the very Deities themfelves. They all fmil'd at the jealous Spite of *Vulcan*, whifpering, that there was not much Prefumption in affecting to be like his Godfhip.

JUPITER, knowing himfelf cenfur'd for not fpending a Thunderbolt or two upon fuch a Race of prefumptuous Animals, faid, *Momus* was in the right, in thinking Mankind fitter to be fcorn'd than punifh'd, for fo ridiculous a Pride, efpecially fince none in that divine Affembly had ever thought it worth their While to inform them better.

MOMUS, thus applauded by *Jove*, ventur'd at deriding the Gods themfelves a little, for fuffering the very worft of Men fometimes to rule over the very beft, in their Name, and as their Vice-gerents: Nay, *Apollo*, ask'd Permiffion, by Way of jefting, to make them Prophets too, as well

as

as Princes; becaufe he doubted fome of them might hardly be able to fpeak Senfe, without the Help of Infpiration.

HOWEVER, they admitted of Exceptions to this general Obfervation about Princes; and efpecially for the Female Sex : Firft, becaufe you muft know the Gods are extreamly well-bred; and next, you may be fure the old merry Saying would not fail to-take, at fuch a jovial Meeting, That of, *Queens being ftill advis'd by* Men, *while Kings are often influenc'd by* Women.

THE Gods being now grown a little tipfy, laugh'd aloud at every thing that *Momus* faid, though his Jefts, as I fear you will find, did not always deferve it.

YET he took Notice right enough of a certain great and politick * Prince, whofe Vanity fo much outweighs his Wifdom, that, inftead of cajoling a proud Nation to change their Mafter, he daily affronts them by fome imperious Novelty or other, either about changing their Garb or Government; for want of confidering, that Pride had rather be punifh'd than flighted.

ANOTHER † Prince, lately deceas'd in Exile, was cenfur'd alfo (yet with great

---

* *Lewis* XIV.   † K. *James* II.

Com-

Compaffion, amidft all their Mirth) becaufe, tho' he not only meant to govern
well, but had Talents capable of it; yet,
notwithftanding all that, he loft three Kingdoms, meerly for want of being wifely
principled in his Youth, and inftructed, that
Kings fhould indeed reverence the Gods,
and appear decently devout, but never violently zealous for any thing befides Juftice,
and the publick Good; which Vertue alone,
they faid, without other Religion, is fufficient to make them Heroes on Earth, and
advance them afterwards to be Demi-Gods
in Heaven.

A L L the Gods admired that odd Mixture of which his † Succeffor was compo-
fed; fo very lazy, heavy, and eafily impos'd
on by Favourites, and yet fo very ambitious
and enterprizing; which they attributed to
the different Characters of his Anceftors;
who, on his Mother's Side, were *only* Sove-
reigns (*Henry* IV. of *France* excepted) but,
on his Father's, fuch as *deferved* to be fo.

Y E T *Jupiter* himfelf fhew'd great Efteem
of him; but was fufpected a little of fome
Partiality, on account of his own Proceedings with old Father *Saturn*. He was ob-

---

† *William* III.

ferved

ferved alfo to kifs *Ganymede* all the while they were talking of this Prince, which made the Gods whifper to one another a litttle malicioufly.

THERE was a certain * King in a Corner, which they had alfo a Fling at, for having made too bold with a Lunatick Brother; and for fuffering his Minifters afterwards to make too bold with himfelf; fo that neither his Subjects, nor Allies, were much the better for his good Intentions. But as to his Brother, *Momus* himfelf excus'd him, faying, all things fhould be judg'd by Comparifon, defiring them to look about the World, and fee how little Nearnefs of Blood was confider'd. Upon being ask'd, if he meant any particular Perfon, he defired to be excus'd for having drank a Cup of *Nectar* too much; then fmiling faid, he wifh'd that Prince fo well, he would advife him to do like the Eaftern Monarchs, and take fome good Phyfician for one of his Minifters.

THERE was a † northern Prince, whom the Gods themfelves hardly knew what to make of; fomething humourfome, very brave, mighty revengeful, indefatigable,

---

* King of *Portugal.* † King of *Sweden.*

and

and violently ambitious; fome of the main
Ingredients that make a Heroe. But, tho'
we Mortals are counted foolifh, who judge
by Succefs; yet the very Gods were forc'd
to do it in this Cafe, and fufpend their
Judgment of this Prince a-while, afham'd
to be puzzled by a Youth of Four and
Twenty.

THEY perceiv'd another ‡ King hard by,
in the fame Quarter, much concern'd for
the Lofs of a * Brother, whom many
Years ago he had difpos'd of extreamly
well; yet no Body fince ever heard one
Word of him. *Momus*, laughing faid, the
good Prince was not quite dead, tho' forc'd
to breathe hard to prevent being buried;
becaufe no Body perceived any other Sign
of Life in him. Some of the Gods fmil'd,
and faid, it would be well for the Quiet
of Mankind, if all Princes were as dull
and infignificant.

ANOTHER † King would fcarce have
been taken Notice of, if he had not, one
Morning, taken that Title for his Morning's Draught, and declar'd himfelf to be
one. But the Gods faid, for his Excufe,
that there was more plain Dealing in that

---

‡ King of *Denmark.*   * Prince *George* of *Denmark.*
† King of *Pruffia.*

Proceeding than in all the reft of that Rank, who pretended to derive theirs, either from the Gods, or Approbation of the People, whereas neither in Reality are the leaft guilty of the Matter.

THIS honeft Prince (faid *Momus*) went more plainly to work; and becaufe no body elfe cared for him enough to do it, even took a good Refolution, and fet up himfelf. *Mars* frown'd, and faid, it was of ill Example, and againft the Cuftom of Princes; whofe additional new Honours and Titles are ever wont to arife from Wars and Conqueft, out of the Blood and Treafure of their Subjects.

BUT *Jupiter* told him he was a bluftering God, to find Fault with the only good Circumftance of fo vain an Action; which yet in time would make his mifchievous Godfhip Amends, by fetting agog all the little Princes both of *Italy* and *Germany*, whofe Mouths now water at the fame Dignity, and, to obtain it, will never let *Europe* be quiet.

NOW came into Play an odd Animal, which *Momus* faid was call'd an Emperor, * juft as a little *Indian* Bird is call'd a Pope,

* *Leopold* Emperor of *Germany*.

only

only becaufe there grows a high Topping upon his Head. Some faid he was above all Kings, only as their Hats are; and that he begg'd every Body's Affiftance, while he would not help himfelf. Some of the Gods faid, they very often indeed vouch-fafed to help poor Mortals who cannot, but never fuch who will not help themfelves. However the Gods admired the odd Zeal of thofe who devoutly preferve their Religion in one Country, and yet at the fame Time affift a Prince who perfecutes the fame Religion in another.

Upon this Occafion, *Jupiter* obferv'd, how filly Mortals prefume to blame Providence for the Weaknefs, or Wickednefs of hereditary Princes, while yet they are not much happier under thofe whom they elect themfelves. This gave *Momus* an Opportunity of Raillery: The double Pretentions to Crowns, fo much in Fafhion now-a-days, arifing moft commonly from the People's fetting up new Princes, becaufe they always fancy thofe beft with whom they are the leaft acquainted.

Some Mention at laft was made of a certain * People remarkable for Induftry,

---

* The *Dutch.*

and

and for having no other good Quality befides ; whom *Momus* yet defended malicioufly enough, by fhewing the great Influence they have over a great and rich Nation,
that has the Folly to be impos'd on by them
both at home and abroad, tho' the dulleft
Creatures alive.

THE Affairs of *Italy* were in too melan-
cholly a Pofture for fuch a Feaft of Jollity;
and the Gods in all their Mirth, were yet
incapable of mocking at † two Princes of
one Houfe in that Country, who make
fo great a Figure there.

ON the contrary, they all declar'd una-
nimoufly, that one of them as much out-
fhin'd all the *Monarchs* of this Age, as the
other excell'd the *Generals*; for which juft
Encomium, not only *Mars*, but *Minerva*
alfo, in juft Gratitude, rofe up, and made
Obeifance to that auguft Affembly.

---

† The Duke of *Savoy*, and Prince *Eugene* of *Savoy*.

FINIS.